HANDBAGS

the ultimate accessory

Tessa
Paul

HANDBAGS

the ultimate accessory

CHARTWELL
BOOKS, INC.

This edition published in 2010 by

CHARTWELL BOOKS, INC.

A Division of
BOOK SALES, INC.
276 Fifth Avenue Suite 206
New York, New York 10001
USA

ISBN-13: 978-0-7858-2592-0
ISBN-10: 0-7858-2592-4

Produced for Compendium Publishing Ltd by:
Editorial Developments
Edgmond
Shropshire
England.

Design by: Chensie Chen

Printed in China

HANDBAGS
CONTENTS

HANDBAGS
INTRODUCTION

The story of the handbag is a fascinating but slow narrative until the twentieth century, when exciting, startling designs burst upon the world of fashion and the purse became an essential part of every woman's wardrobe.

In his book *A History of Costume* (1871), Carl Köhler points out that generally "fashions retain styles and forms of cut that really belong to periods long past (these are technically called 'fossils') and . . . connecting threads from distant centuries persist into modern times." His words scarcely make sense in the twenty-first century, where "fossil" wear is unknown. We live in a world where many women can afford to buy gorgeous, high-fashion handbags.

But it is as well to remember that until the twentieth century almost every single man-made object, from wheels to chairs, from hats to skirts to purses, was handmade. It took time and skill to produce anything, so objects and clothes were kept carefully, mended when necessary, and everything was expected to remain in use for many, many years. The poor and underprivileged workers did not respond to fashion: they could not afford to do so.

This book tells the story of the function of the purse and its offspring, the handbag, and studies the beautiful designs lavished on this accessory. Through the colors, the decoration, and the materials, it is possible to trace not only historic fashions and social manners, but also the inexorable progress of technology.

LEFT: Despite the seemingly casual outfit of shorts and loose layers of shirt and jacket, this fashion model wears an impressive bag of silvered leather. The accessory has been elevated to make the most important statement in her outfit.

HANDBAGS

Human beings have always been designers as well as makers. Fragments of textiles and leather dug from archeological sites of great age show patterns formed by beads or stitching. Purses revealed in historic mosaics, frescoes, and manuscripts give proof of sophisticated ornament and beautifully controlled handicraft.

But it was only in the twentieth century that bag designers were acknowledged and credited. Some of these talented people became household names, recognized for their infallible artistic sense and creative purpose. In the following we discuss, decade by decade, the work and contribution of the most famous designers. We also trace the changing styles of the purse, the accessory that women rely on to update and enhance every outfit.

Yet the handbag is more than the ultimate accessory: it is the portable holder of life as women know it. Here are stored all the most intimate requirements of a woman's world—cosmetics, toiletries, diaries, address books, letters, credit cards, cell phone, keys to home, car, and office. Designers vie with each other to create this object, which is secretive, intimate, and yet very public. Women will spend great sums on the perfect bag, one that makes a status statement while giving subtle signs of the wearer's personality.

RIGHT: Contemporary high-end handbag manufacturers are fully integrated into department stores. Even when they have their own retail outlets, a dedicated space in a superior store attracts many customers. The famous names of Gucci and Vuitton are boldly displayed across the general purse department of this store.

bags ...

The story turns even more interesting with the approach of the twenty-first century. Beautiful handbags have become available to many women, as the designs aimed at the elite are easily reproduced at an economical price. Colors, decoration, and fabric are available in an exciting array, and the rich are no longer the only dedicated followers of fashion.

Those women constantly searching for the perfect purse will be delighted to follow the history of design and fashion recounted in this book. They will also able to feast their eyes on the superb color photographs that show both the historic and the contemporary handbag in all its lovely detail.

LEFT: Many women may regard this image as sacrilegious. After all, the purse offers a private, even a secret, place for the intimate essentials of life, yet here they are—money, cosmetics, jewels, keys, photos, everything—spilled out and displayed for the public gaze!

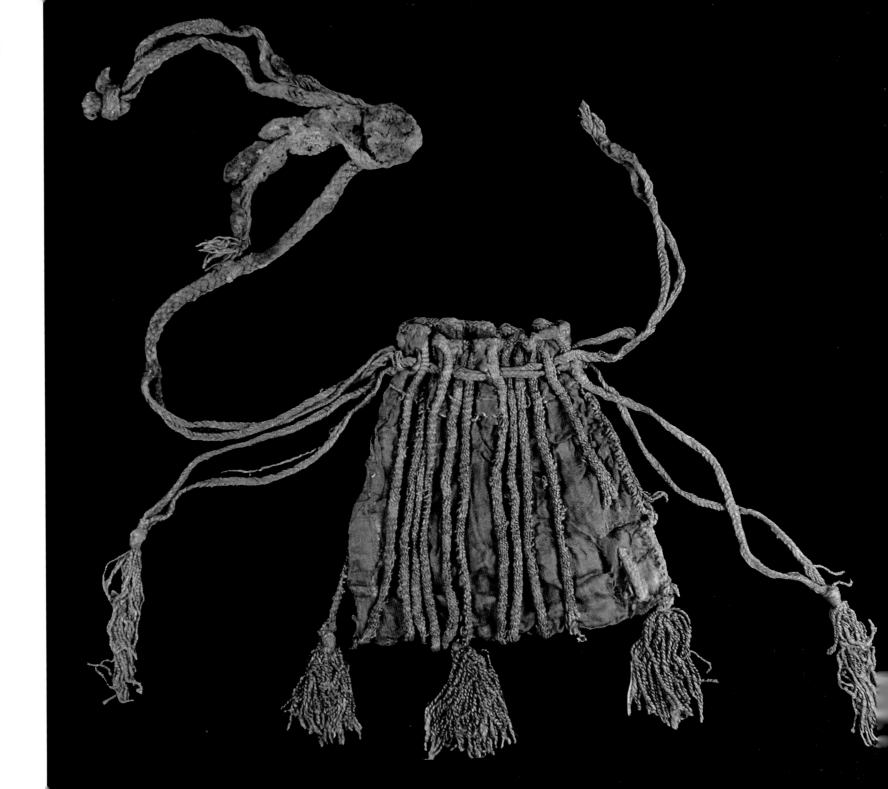

STORY OF THE
HANDBAG

Handbags and purses are everyday, practical items, yet they have provoked some unexpected responses. Early feminists derided them as symbols of female vanity and appeasement, while Freudians analyze the female sexual symbolism of the handbag—its firm clasp, its secret interior. In seventeenth-century slang, the word "purse" was used as a rude name applied to women, and when Mrs Thatcher, Britain's first female prime minister, came to office, the noun became a verb: to "handbag" someone was to bully them.

But bags were born from necessity, and for centuries were used by both men and women. Before mankind had animals of burden, food, implements, seeds, and weapons needed to be transported from one place to another, so it can be assumed that pre-historic hunter-gatherer nomads required bags. These objects have not survived the ravages of time, but modern hunter-gatherers like the Bushmen (Koi Koi) of Southern Africa carry their few possessions and food by knotting their *karosses*, cloaks made of animal skin, into large pouches.

LEFT: Perhaps the earliest bags were formed by pouching a length of leather and tying it at the neck with a cord, and then later, the cord was attached by threading it through slots at the neck. So, the drawstring bag was made. This one dates from the thirteenthth century. It is basic in design yet it is interesting to see the craftsman could not resist adding a little artistry in making decorative cords and tassels.

However, it is safe to assume the first actual purses were simple drawstring pouches, or lengths of leather folded into an envelope. In Ancient Egyptian artwork there are images of men with bags, or purses hanging from their belts. *The Bible* describes the treacherous tax collector, Judas Iscariot, as a "purse-carrier."

LEFT: Remains of a purse from the early fifteenth century. The original folded leather envelope has been opened and flattened, but the cut-out on the upper edge indicates that once a clasp held the folded leather.

There is evidence that the fifth-century warriors of Attila the Hun carried their arrows in stiff oblong bags tied to their belts, and there is an extant Scythian leather pouch from the same era. In medieval images and texts, we find further evidence of the purse. These were tied or slotted onto the belt or sometimes fitted with a strap slung across the chest. Men and women wore purses in these ways so their hands were free to handle livestock, children, food, tools, and weapons.

ABOVE: This scene from the Biblical story of "The Prodigal Son" is a part of the Sheldon Tapestries dated c.1600. It illustrates the elderly father, seated, as he greets his wayward boy by offering the gift of a deep moneybag.

15

But, of course, the bag moved beyond its function, and its form began to convey the prestige of the wearer. Big, bulky bags were the sign of a peasant and hard, physical labor while charming little purses decorated with fancy metalwork or fine embroidery signified the leisured, moneyed classes. The rich and powerful had no need to haul round tools or animal feed, but used purses to stow their money, rosaries, and pomades.

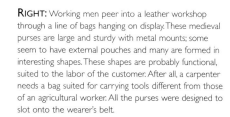

LEFT: A medieval Persian hunter is shown carrying his arrows in a stiff, long, and narrow bag, which is attached to his saddle. The bag is similar to the kind that would have been used by Attila the Hun. For many centuries, this style of arrow bag was used all over Central Asia.

RIGHT: Working men peer into a leather workshop through a line of bags hanging on display. These medieval purses are large and sturdy with metal mounts; some seem to have external pouches and many are formed in interesting shapes. These shapes are probably functional, suited to the labor of the customer. After all, a carpenter needs a bag suited for carrying tools different from those of an agricultural worker. All the purses were designed to slot onto the wearer's belt.

Fortunately for historians, Renaissance purses have survived as hard proof of the form and function of these objects. In the Victoria and Albert Museum, London, one of the earliest examples is the Calthorpe Purse, made, it is estimated, in about 1540 and the museum also has examples of metalwork on early purses.

Since ancient times, metalworkers have been part of European culture, making armor and numerous domestic items such as locks, doorknobs —and purses. Purse mounts were stamped with patterns while the clasps were moulded into intricate shapes. In the Metropolitan Museum, New York, there is a fifteenth century purse with an iron clasp shaped as a tiny castle.

RIGHT: The Calthorpe Purse is an important historic artifact in the fashion collection of the Victoria and Albert Museum. The charming patchwork effect is designed to represent the coats of arms of the Calthorpe family.

LEFT: The Calthorpe Purse is worked in tent stitch and the colors, though varied and now faded, were determined by the family's ancient heraldic symbols. The handiwork is delicate, using about 1,250 stitches per square inch.

Leather could carry metal ornament, but small purses made of silk or linen were not suited to the weight of metal. They could be ornamented with mother-of-pearl or enamel medallions, but needlework was the preferred method of decorating these textiles. Embroidery is an old craft that probably started in the East. The use of different threads and stitches gives texture and shape: metal threads, for instance, are rich in both qualities while also conveying the wealth of the owner. Embroidery allows an infinite variety of design in color, words, and images on fabric. Purses, usually small in size, are ideal for this craft of intricate detail. Needle-craft from the sixteenth and seventeenth centuries show texts, symbolic plants, and heraldic symbols.

LEFT: The detail shown in this section of the bag is of a man with a dog. The animal signifies loyalty and no doubt the man represents a beloved figure in the embroiderer's life.

These small purses were treasured items, given as gifts or to mark betrothals. Not all were designed as receptacles for money and the like, but to store jewels or phials of perfume. The embroidered purses were so beautiful, with drawstrings of plaited silk ending in silver bobbles and soft tassels that they became keepsakes, treasured by families down the years. Perhaps this is why so many examples have survived—such purses were rarely ruined by constant use.

LEFT: Small, neat, with its pleats held in place by the stiffness of the gilt stitching, the gaming purse was for the dandy gambler. The base identifies the aristocratic owner. The stitching on this example is very intricate and, perhaps, was worked by an adoring maiden but, just as likely, the nobleman employed embroiderers among his domestic staff.

RIGHT: For centuries, embroidery was the most easily available decoration for textiles, and skill at needlework was common across all levels of society. This section of a pocket purse and its intricate embroidery is from the sixteenth century and is reputed to have been stitched by the doomed Mary, Queen of Scots.

For the leisured aristocracy, small gaming purses appeared, constructed with a firm circular base and tied by drawstring. These purses were stiff with metal thread and pearls. Often the owner was identified by the coat of arms embroidered on the base. The interiors were fitted with circular compartments to hold coins and counters.

The embroiderers were usually the wife and daughters of the house, but the very rich included embroiderers among their household staff. Even so, every well-bred young woman knew her needlework. (Mary, Queen of Scots depended on embroidery to while away the hours during her long imprisonment.) Yet not every household had the time to make purses, and merchants could be found selling them in markets and even traveling round villages in search of customers.

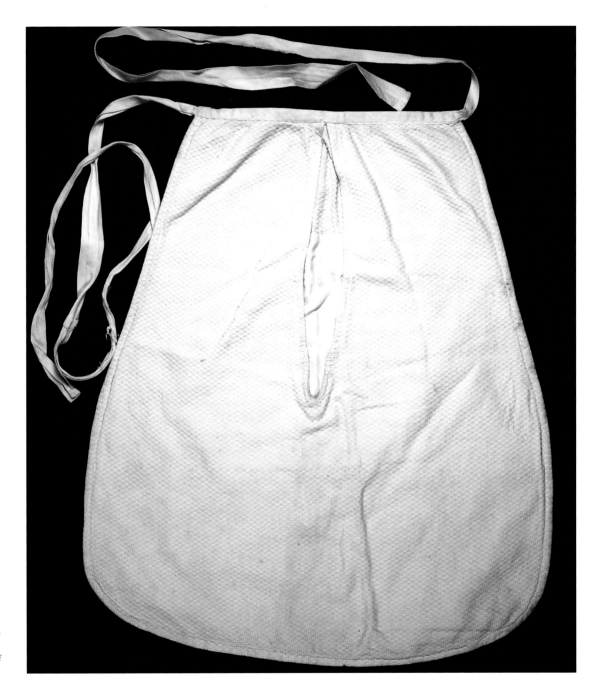

RIGHT: A white linen pocket purse hints at a woman who, perhaps, preferred the minimalist style. More likely, she had neither the time nor inclination to embroider a garment that was hidden from the public eye and was not going to serve as an indication of her social status.

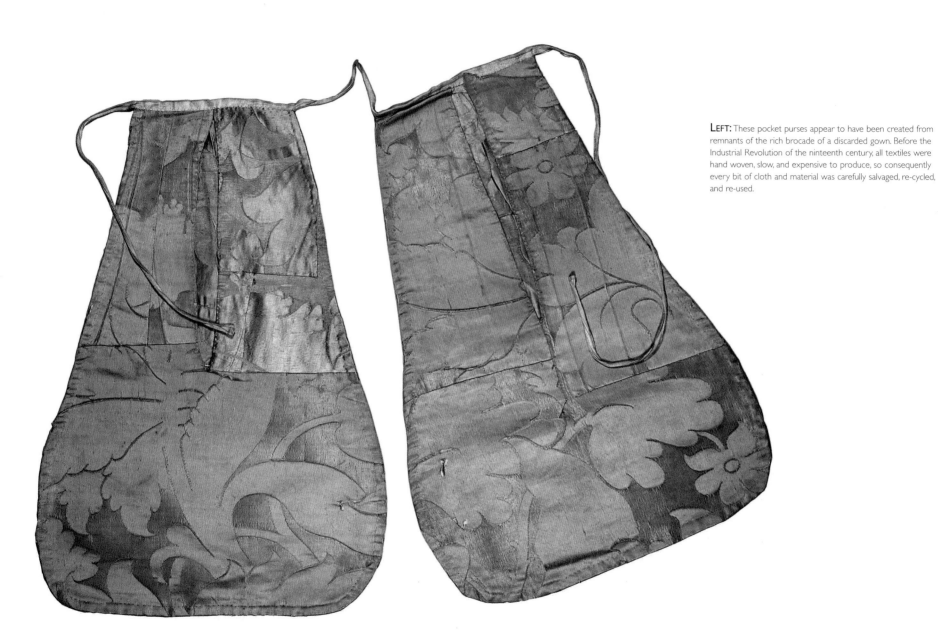

LEFT: These pocket purses appear to have been created from remnants of the rich brocade of a discarded gown. Before the Industrial Revolution of the ninteenth century, all textiles were hand woven, slow, and expensive to produce, so consequently every bit of cloth and material was carefully salvaged, re-cycled, and re-used.

Purse makers experimented with textiles and ornamentation but purses remained small: noble women were obliged to secrete large personal possession in muffs. Gradually, though, women's purses grew into large drawstring workbags attached to the belt.

Pockets on clothing were introduced in the mid-sixteenth century, and by the seventeenth century pockets were part of male—though not of female—clothing. Women wore pocket purses: two pockets were stitched to a long ribbon tied around the waist over the petticoat and spaced so that each pocket fitted over each hip. Skirts were made with slits so that the wearer could reach her hand into her "pocket."

LEFT: Beadwork, like embroidery, is a form of decoration suited to the size of a handbag but it has the advantage of giving the bag weight and form. This pouch has a name worked into the decoration so, probably, it was intended as a gift. It dates from the seventeenth century.

LEFT: The decoration on early purses was not merely ornamental, but also meaningful. In this detail, two figures carry flames, perhaps to indicate warmth and passion. Is the smaller figure that of Cupid, the messenger of love? People of the seventeenth century were familiar with such symbols, but we must assume this beaded bag carries a message of courtship.

The pocket purses were prettily embroidered and usefully large. In 1667 a description of a noble woman's belongings listed that "her ample pockets abounded in dainty implements." Such women kept their fans, needlework, money, keys, and household lists in their "ample pockets."

RIGHT: This letter wallet is typical of the ware produced by Turkish craftsmen for tourists. These men were renowned for their fine leatherwork. This example shows silver and gold metal threads skilfully stitched to give an intricate surface on the leather, and the embroidered city name was a little extra to persuade travelers to buy the wallet as a souvenir of their visit.

By the eighteenth century, pockets were a regular part of male clothing and men were persuaded to use pocket cases or "lettercases" of leather or fine textiles. Each case was a narrow clutch that folded out into a long, flat rectangle to reveal compartments designed to hold visiting cards and bank bills. Lettercases were worn in the pocket and quickly became a symbol of wealth, signified by lavish embroidery on silk or the softest leather. These cases may have been introduced from the Ottoman Empire brought to Europe by travelers. The housewives of Europe made lettercases as betrothal presents, embroidered with symbols of love, hearts, and cupids, or images of little dogs signifying steadfast loyalty. Gilt thread and pearls added to the real and metaphorical value of these gifts.

LEFT: This embroidered purse has been thoughtfully designed and beautifully stitched. Each animal and plant carries symbolic value and, as is usual with these historic embroidered purses, the patient handicraft and the motifs used indicate the making of a precious betrothal gift.

The large workbag came back into use in the late eighteenth century. These were traditional drawstring bags but now housed the needlework implements that every fashionable woman carried about with her. Sewing was an accepted social activity and women would continue their handiwork even when visiting their neighbors. The workbag held her embroidery threads, scissors, and shuttles for knotting, a form of weaving used to make braids to trim purses.

LEFT: For those women who could afford it, fashionable dressing was a major preoccupation—as it always has been and as, no doubt, always will be. This smart young woman carries a reticule that has been made from the same fabric as her long coat. It is attached to a metal mount. These were mass produced for individuals, as well as stores, to purchase. We can assume her dressmaker created this bespoke ensemble, bag and all.

Domestic handiwork was helped by industrial developments. By the late eighteenth century, ready-made metal mounts with top closings were available in the stores, and pattern books provided thousands of needlework designs for the home needle worker. Advanced glass technology developed a way of making beads in vast quantities, and needle workers used these to embellish their embroidery.

Fashion underwent a radical change at the beginning of the nineteenth century. Women were persuaded to wear narrow frocks, known as the Empire style, and purses were modified to suit this "new look." Pocket purses could not be hidden under the skirt and the empire dress had no belt, so the fashionista had to carry her purse: which by this time was called a reticule.

LEFT: Pattern books were available for embroiderers, but the work on this pretty reticule is not as complex as those from earlier times. The design is comparatively simple and the stitching less refined. It hints that the effects of the machine-made and mass-produced were beginning to corrode traditional household crafts.

RIGHT: Berlin work, quick and easy to stitch, was used on big, deep bags. They were worked in strong colors and further embellished with fancy cords and tassels. The boldness of Berlin work is difficult to match with a girlish evening dress.

Reticules were hung from the wrist on long drawstring cords but they were not always the simple pouch shape of old. Mechanization made lightweight silver frames or bases over which the home worker could stretch or pleat textiles. The surfaces were decorated with embroidery, beads, and fringes. The ready-made metal mounts were prettily stamped, and chains or fabric handles were attached to links on the mount.

Throughout the nineteenth century, Berlin woolwork, demanding less skill than embroidery, grew in popularity. Housewives began to use this craft to decorate their purses, slippers, and stool covers. Wool was stitched onto canvas, and thousands of easy-to-follow designs were printed to meet the demand. New advances in color dyes for textiles added to the excitement of Berlin woolwork, and designs became bold in both color and concept. Because canvas does not gather smoothly onto a drawstring, the purses were given long, corded handles with elaborate tassels.

THE CHATELAINE ; A REALLY USEFUL PRESENT.

Laura. "OH! LOOK, MA' DEAR; SEE WHAT A *LOVE* OF A CHATELAINE EDWARD HAS GIVEN ME."

LEFT: Chatelaines have a busy, efficient appearance but many were merely decorative. Scissors, sewing materials, and memo books were beautifully fitted and designed, and the whole was attached to the belt with a decorative clasp. As the nineteenth century drew to a close, the chatelaine had been transformed into a leather bag from which dangled chains adorned with charming, but essentially useless household tools. Maintaining the pretense that the chatelaine was an essential item to the housewife, never to be put aside, the bag continued to be attached to the belt.

Victorian women started to hang their household necessities from their belts. Keys, scissors, pin cushion, sewing implements, memo book, a phial of perfume, a coin purse—all now dangled on chains from the housewife's waist, and all were factory-made. These arrangements came to be called *chatelaines*. The very name shows the pretension behind the new wealth of the Industrial Revolution, and the recent emergence of the middle-class housewife. The French name means "lady of the castle."

RIGHT: The porters played an important role at the first railroad stations. They transported the huge amount of luggage brought by each passenger and stored it in a special luggage van. On the trolley there is a very large leather suitcase and a capacious carpetbag in Berlin work, both common sights on the busy platforms of large stations at the end of the nineteenth century.

The railroad may be seen as the invention that brought the most radical change to the design and use of bags and purses. Railroads allowed journeys that few had bothered to take previously, when travel by horse and coach was slow and pricey.

Now more and more people took to traveling long distances and they needed large purses to carry money, handiwork, tickets, papers, and even clothing. Domestic purse makers responded by stitching large travel bags in Berlin woolwork and these became known as "carpet bags."

LEFT: The wealthy did not travel lightly on the early railroads. Their wardrobes were complicated and demanded a lot of luggage. Here, a lady's maid guards numerous bags and trunks, but she carries a large handbag, shaped as a small suitcase, designed especially for the female traveler. This is probably the maid's own possession.

I, RUE SCRIBE,
PARIS.

Louis Vuitton

149, NEW BOND ST.
OPPOSITE CONDUIT ST.
LONDON, W.

TELEGRAPHIC ADDRESS,
"VUITTON, LONDON."
TELEPHONE Nº 2587, GERARD.

Travelling Requisites

LEFT: The family company of Louis Vuitton was quick to respond to the new traveler—the passenger on the railroads. This is the cover of their English catalogue dated 1901. They made trunks, suitcases, and handbags in both canvas and leather. So successful were the Italian company in the early twentieth century, that they opened branches in London and Paris.

BELOW: The famous Louis Vuitton Steamer bag was first made in 1901. Its success lay in part because the handle was designed to fit the size of a woman's hand and the base to sit securely on a cabin door handle. The company continues to manufacture variations on this superbly designed and much admired bag.

But the leather craftsmen also spotted the need for large, sturdy travel equipment. By the late nineteenth century, workshops once dedicated to making saddles and other items for horses turned to producing travel luggage. By the end of the century, manufacturers began to produce bags for women to pack their essentials for overnight travel.

The interior of the female travel bag was fitted with various compartments to hold cosmetics, perfumes, brushes, and the like. Initially, the servants carried these; rich women did not haul luggage about but still, the lady required a purse for money and tickets—the handbag was born. Now, the fashionable woman carried a soft pouch or a chic firm rectangle, made in leather with chrome clasps and mounts and with short leather handles.

LEFT: Generally, every woman owned a large drawstring workbag, but a clever manufacturer produced this workbag designed for ultimate convenience. The firm base could be settled on a table or on the floor, yet look stylish and remain stable. Often the base was constructed from papier mâché and given a textile covering.

HANDBAGS

These resembled small travel bags with pockets for cosmetics, money, opera glasses, and fans. Some even resembled workmen's bags with a shoulder sling worn across the chest although conservatives found this a vulgar development. When steamship travel became voguish, Louis Vuitton made a "Steamer" bag in 1901 of soft leather with leather mounts closed by a strap and buckle. The handles were designed to hang on the back of a steamship cabin door.

RIGHT: This evening purse is made of fine metal mesh and probably came from a jeweler. It has an unusual closure: half the bag's opening is threaded onto a bangle handle; the other half is folded and closed by a tasselled "button." These limp and flexible small mesh bags were well matched to the tubular, beaded cocktail dresses fashionable at the time.

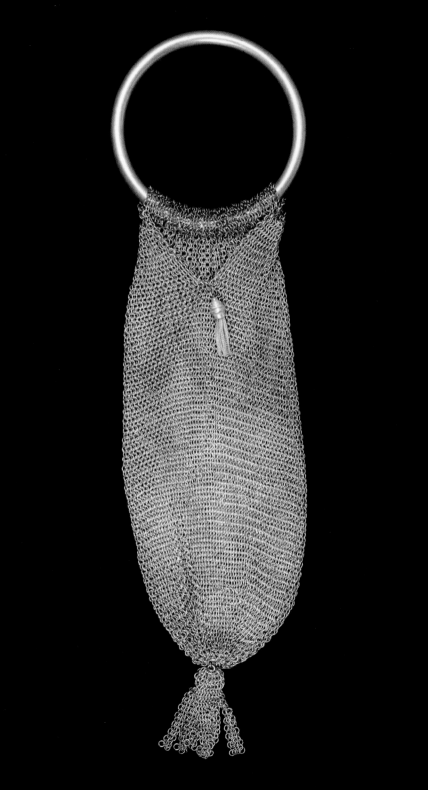

Jewelry makers quickly took advantage of the new handbag. At the turn of the twentieth century, smart little handbags, bejeweled miracles of engineering, were created for the glamorous women of high society. The bags were made of fur, worked leather, bright silks, satins, and velvets. Others were made of chain-linked silver or similar metal materials.

LEFT: At last, handbags had grown up and could assume any role whether useful, decorative, frivolous, or sensible. Manufacturers widened their range of products, moving beyond leather, canvas, and the small suitcase bag. This purse refers to historic styles, while mixing mass production with handicraft. It retains the age-old drawstring construction and embroidered decoration while adding unexpected flaps.

Decorative mounts and clasps were devised using fine metals and expensive gemstones. Carved ivory and tortoiseshell were favored as were metal lace and gold threads. The insides of these bags carried discrete compartments for powder compacts, opera glasses, and money purses. Such items were made to match the handbag, being worked from the same fabric and carrying similar ornament.

LEFT: Women demanded pretty bags for formal wear. This mix of velvet and silver metal was popular at the turn of the twentieth century and shows a move from the abundant decoration so loved by the Victorians. The markings on the metal mount are understated; this is a mass produced object and has a neat unobtrusive clasp.

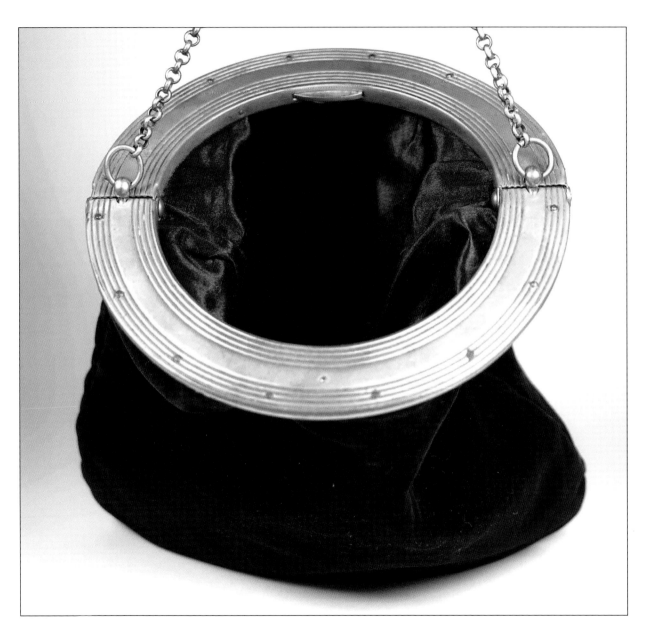

Women were enjoying unheard-of freedom of movement, unguarded by men or chaperones. Women travelled alone and went to work, so handbags became essential to haul around tickets, money, cosmetics, magazines and umbrellas. Louis Vuitton and Hermès made sleek bags that doubled as travel bag and handbag.

LEFT: The deep interior of the bag is silky but able to withstand light objects such as a small bottle of perfume. In the evening, women of class were chaperoned by fathers, husbands, or brothers who took care of money and keys. Also, respectable women did not wear make-up; the paraphernalia of powder compacts, lipstick, and so on were as yet unknown to them.

When the twentieth century began, handbags were firmly established as an essential part of every woman's wardrobe. The modern age was to see the development of mass production and the spread of wealth that changed a utility item—the handbag—into a joyous and frivolous necessity for women everywhere.

LEFT: The wealthy could afford dinky little purses, with silver mounts fitted with semi-precious stones and interiors holding intricate compartments. Less fortunate women had access to more prosaic designs, but it was still possible to find mounts that were handsome, and rich-looking fabrics adorned with embroidery, every bit as pretty as gems.

RIGHT: Small glass beads add gleam and glitter; pleats add interest to the pouch, and a chain handle brings panache to this handbag.

1920s
STYLE AND LIBERTY

Every war brings advances in technology, and the mechanical weapons and vehicles used in the First World War motivated scientists. They refined metals, rubber, plastics, and synthetic fabrics. These improvements affected the civilian world, including the fashion sector. Plastic could be used as a substitute for metals and animal products, rayon, and rubber were so refined they could be used in clothing. For instance, smooth and elastic rubber made a comfortable girdle, much nicer than the tightly laced, uncomfortable, whale-boned corsets of the pre-war years.

And women who had spent the war wearing factory overalls or practical pants for ambulance driving were in no mood for tight corsets, elaborate skirts, and huge hats, outfits that inhibited movement. Besides, a reckless mood overtook the generation who survived the conflict. Having lived through harsh events that destroyed any belief in an ordered, predictable future, many young men and women plunged into wild hedonism, rejecting the values of the generation that had taken them into war. The cultural upheaval affected all aspects of society in ways that are perhaps difficult for later generations to understand.

LEFT: The mood after the Great War was determinedly cheerful. Hemlines no longer swept the ankle and technical advances brought new synthetic fabrics. Handmade handbags were no longer the norm, and women revelled in mass-produced clutch purses, or those with a short, single strap to hook over the wrist.

45

In art, architecture, and music, the younger generation drew inspiration from peasant Russia, Ancient Egypt, and Africa. The tomb of the Egyptian pharaoh, Tutankhamun, was opened in 1922 and Europe responded stylistically to the artistic strangeness of the ancient hieroglyphics and frescoes uncovered by the archaeologists.

This Egyptian art presents a stylized representation of people, outlined in black, colored in reds and greens, and unlike anything seen before in the West. The formal, vertical placing of images creates a pattern that excited the artistic world, and the influence of Ancient Egypt could be seen in fabric design and the decorated leather of handbags. The general public were fascinated by the story of Tutankhamun. Sure of a ready sale, manufacturers produced purses and wallets covered in reproductions of Egyptian art.

LEFT: Beaded evening handbags are a perennial favorite. This example from France gives a small nod to ornament with a beaded handle and an engraved metal mount.

ABOVE: Designers of the '20s were inspired by exotic artistic traditions. This European interpretation of an Oriental style relies more on obvious images of Chinese people than actually copying the work of their artists. Nevertheless, this handbag is hand embroidered and charming.

LEFT: Russian folk art favors fat flowers and warm colors. This purse replicates, in metallic thread, the paintings found on Russian bowls, cups, and plates that in the ninteenth century used to be made of papier mâché.

But designers and craftsmen were equally thrilled by the colorful, fantastic costumes of the Ballet Russes that visited Paris after the war. Oriental and folk art made, they believed, a fascinating mix. The ballet costumes were designed by Léon Bakst. He interpreted traditional peasant needlework, bringing a swirling line and bold color to the old designs of plant and animal forms. His bright, joyous costumes were rapidly absorbed by the fashion world.

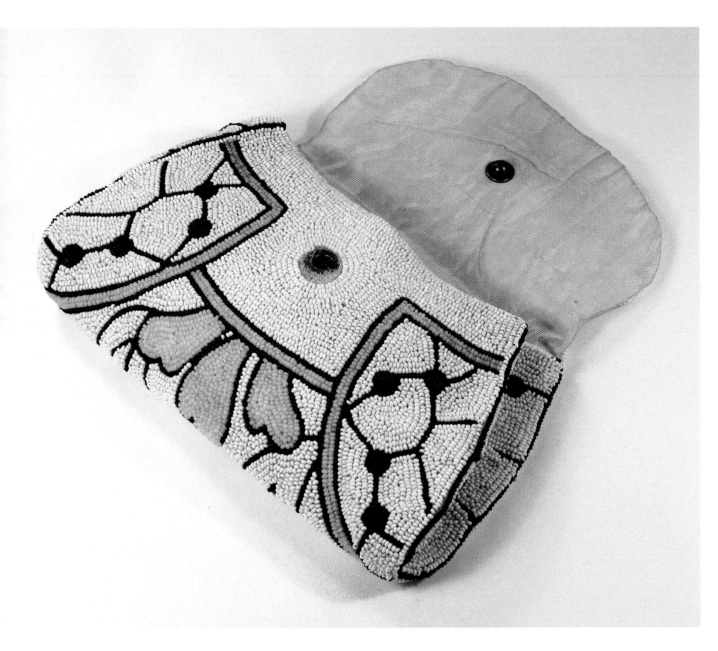

Thanks to the camera, explorers captured images of African fetish objects and brought back to Europe wooden carvings of angular, unexpected beauty. Even more exciting to fashionable society was the arrival of African-American dancers and jazzmen. The female Americans, in particular, enjoyed great freedom in their dance and the lyrics of their songs. The young in Paris and New York were entranced by the exuberant and uninhibited style of these entertainers. Traditional European manners were abandoned.

Artists wanted to express the machine age of speed and mechanization. Paintings reflected the sleek lines of cars and planes, while in furniture and architecture, any useless superfluous ornament was banished. People who are now recognized as modern masters were regarded as dangerous revolutionaries in the early twentieth century. The Cubist paintings of Picasso and Braque were incomprehensible to most people but were admired by fashionable youth. The spare buildings of Corbusier and the stern, unornamented architecture of the Bauhaus group in Germany replaced the grandly ornate pillars and façades of Edwardian architecture. The stark new constructions were shocking and the post-war generation loved them.

LEFT: Sparse lines and stark patterning replaced Edwardian detail and curved forms. African art with its abstract rendering of nature and the human form encouraged Western designers to use a simplified approach to their own work. This handbag is an early example of this influence.

RIGHT: It's impossible, now, to fully understand the amazement and thrill caused by the machinery of the early twentieth century. Then, the automobile and the plane were astonishing. This motorcar purse was made, perhaps, to woo a modern young lady and, like the courtship purses of the seventeenth century, these novelty purses were not used often but treasured as a whimsical gift. Similar novelty bags regained popularity in the late twentieth century when handbag models of everyday things appeared, generally covered in gems and crystals. This witty example was made in Germany.

Louis
Vuitton

LEFT: This is a canvas and leather version of the classic Vuitton Papillon bag. It has a leather interior and leather straps, is fitted with golden links, and can be carried in the hand or on the shoulder. Of course, it carries the traditional all-over logo patterning so loved by all Vuitton's clients. This traditional design is subtle but unmistakable, and provides an enviable statement of the wearer's status.

BELOW: When Louis Vuitton opened his workshop on the Asnières-sur-Seine (now Haute-de-Seine) in Paris, he determined to develop a high reputation for innovative design. This fine building is now a private museum holding the long history of the company. The scene depicted here is of a Louis Vuitton delivery van on the Grand Rue in Asnières.

From its beginnings, the Vuitton company catered for the world of leisure, and even now is associated with horseback riding and sailing. Louis Vuitton Malletier opened his leather workshop in Paris in 1854. He was well connected because Princess Eugenie had once employed him and he was able to attract wealthy customers for his high quality products. His early commercial success came with his flat-bottomed travel trunk made of canvas. By the beginning of the First World War, there were Vuitton branches in Great Britain, South America, and Egypt.

Vuitton handbags are designed for both beauty and utility. The Keep-All and Noë styles are classics. In 2001 the company's reputation soared when the designer Marc Jacobs reworked these classics with innovative decoration. His promotion of luxury Vuitton products has made the company a giant in the handbag business.

LEFT: Although relentless marketing has made its name familiar across the world, the Vuitton company retains an elite status for the products carrying its famous name. The ambience of refined taste and craftsmanship is reflected in the current premises of the Vuitton outlet in Paris.

RIGHT: Dresses were short and unstructured, and the strong influence of Chanel can be seen in the outfit worn by the woman in the center. It is narrow and unfussy in its line. Suddenly, a big handbag looked wrong, so small neat purses on thin chains or clutches became the vogue.

A similar artistic revolution occurred in women's clothes, especially in the designs of Coco Chanel. Before the war, long draped skirts, tight waistlines, and huge feather boas were the norm. Chanel introduced minimal mannish outfits, suited to active and independent women. (New rubber undergarments allowed women to wear narrow, body-skimming dresses.)

BELOW: Not every woman threw convention to the wind and, while willing to carry a fashionable clutch, exotic pattern and color was a step too far. This white satin, held in a jewel-like metal mount, made an elegant evening accessory.

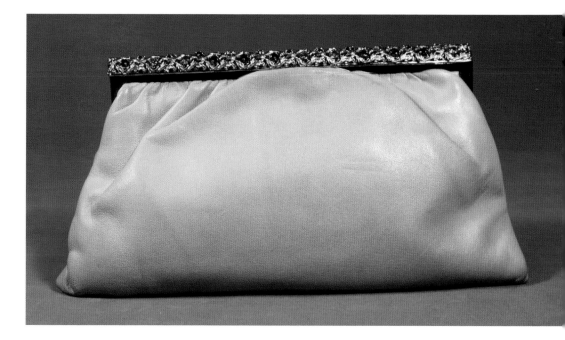

ABOVE: Painting underwent a radical change in the early twentieth century. Realistic representation was abandoned. Dreamlike images, flat color, nature reduced to pattern, rough hatching to indicate shade—all these methods were practiced. Japanese art had these characteristics and its influence can be seen in the fabric used in this French handbag.

Women liked these sexy, flimsy garments that emphasized their mood of liberation. They raised their hemlines and cut their hair short. These changes were truly horrifying to those accustomed to long-haired women, subdued by heavy skirts. These were the days when "a glimpse of stocking was something shocking," so the young had great fun breaking many society taboos and scandalizing their elders.

RIGHT: The robust, strong stitches used on this handbag are a radical interpretation of the delicacy hitherto found in embroidery. The design has a haphazard air, entirely suitable to the prevailing mood of daring and frivolity. Held against a pale evening dress, this purse made a positive statement of modernity.

Handbags reflected the mood of individualism. They were colorful and decorative, and not chosen to "match" an outfit. Fabric pouches were made of densely patterned brocades, old Victorian fabrics, or embroidery, although the needlework was often Chinese. Traditional floral designs were banished. Naïve folk patterns, abstract stripes, and Cubist shapes brought a smart transformation to the *pochette*, or lettercase, now called the clutch. Clasps of carved ivory and metal were adorned with jewels although "simuli"—faux ivory—and plastic often replaced these materials. The synthetics were admired as representing the new world of high technology.

LEFT: This severe metal clutch would have pleased Chanel who, above all, preferred minimal ornament, or even none at all. This clutch complements the uncluttered lines of her 1920s clothing designs. It shows, also, an uncompromising statement of modernity.

Chanel's slim skirts, simple jersey tops, and jackets demanded minimal handbags. The clutch made the perfect accessory: it is narrow and angular in shape, complemented by brightly colored fabric forming geometric patterns. These clutches were held under the upper arm, or the hand was slipped through a flat handle fixed along the back of the bag. Either way, the modern, slim silhouette was not disturbed.

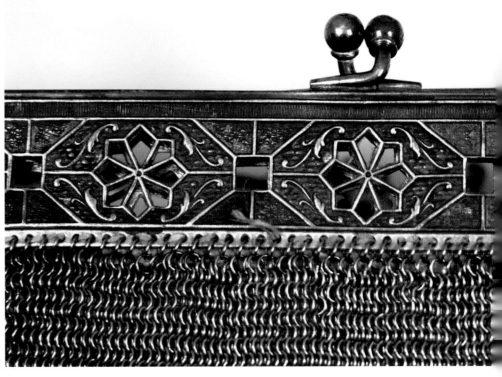

Evening clutches came in hard, shiny plastics with chrome mounts, although jewelers such as Tiffany and Cartier designed clutches that combined valuable gems and precious metals, the interiors engineered to hold lipsticks and cigarette cases. Also, there was a rage for soft, narrow pouches of fine metal mesh, silver or silver plate, suitable for sleek evening clothes. The mounts were patterned and sometimes had jeweled clasps. Mesh bags had a strap worn looped on the wrist, in the style of a reticule.

LEFT: Here is a good example of a firm mount, from which the mesh is held. This reveals a design that hints at the circles, zigzags, and angular shapes of the Art Deco movement that reached its peak in the following decade, the 1930s. It was commissioned by the American store, Whiting and Davis.

RIGHT: Beadwork in subtle grays, silvers, and pinks are not the harsh colors of Art Deco, but the pattern shows the signs of this style. The broad blank areas, divided by geometric lines and abstract floral motifs are typical. The drawstring closure is suitable for the soft but heavy fall of beadwork.

Hermès

RIGHT: Described as a "Modèle Kléber," this is a beautiful example of a 1937 bag presented by Hermès.

Thierry Hermès opened a harness workshop in Paris 1837, and created the first wrought iron bridles and harnesses for horses. In 1880 his son, Charles-Emile, introduced saddlery to the workshop. Thus the pair had the skills to produce luggage for travelers on the new railroads and steam ships. Initially, they concentrated on trunks, but soon turned their attention to bags designed to please women. All their products were handcrafted from the best natural materials.

Hermès remains a family business, and for years all products were made by hand. This tradition made survival difficult in the high-tech world of the twentieth century, and in the 1970s Hermès moved into mass production. Quality remains important, and the classic handbags are still hand-stitched because there is a steady market for them. Hermès does not advertise, but sells on its reputation for craftsmanship and robust design.

LEFT: Hermès conveys an aloof manner, far removed from the hurley-burley of the market place. The company deserves its lofty position for its consistently elegant, well-crafted handbags. These are truly heirloom pieces that will last generations. This is because the designs are timeless and robust in their craftsmanship, as exemplified by this 2009 example.

RIGHT: The Hermès store in Paris, France, can be found on the Rue du Faubourg Saint-Honoré. It occupies a large corner in a prestigious area of high-end retailers and boutiques.

Fine beadwork was used to imitate the shape and fall of the metal mesh reticules. These were worked in colored beads, creating designs of angular, stylized plant forms or geometric patterns. Often they were fringed and carried about in the manner of a Georgian reticule.

RIGHT: The glitter of this French pouch and the patterning capture the mood of the "Roaring Twenties." Silver and gold epitomize the wealth of the Bright Young Things, and the easy, curved lines of the pattern matched unconventional attitudes and the beaded fabrics young women favored in their formal wear.

On the street, the Edwardian handbag that imitated a small travel bag proved to have an enduring appeal. Deeper than it was wide, with a sturdy handle, it was chosen for going to the office or shopping. The best were well-polished quality leather with unobtrusive plastic handles and adornments of chrome strips. Handbags for motoring held compacts and lipsticks.

LEFT: The shape, colors and fabric pattern of this evening purse are traditional, as is the mount. However, before the Industrial Revolution this object would have taken months and numerous craftsmen to make. The weaver, the ironmonger, and the seamstress would all have been involved. The fact that a machine could produce quickly many identical pretty bags was a source of delight to fashion followers of the 1920s. The Mendalion Company is the maker of this typical example of a metallic purse.

LEFT: Strenuous sport played by women in public was a comparatively new development. The French Wimbledon champion, Suzette Lenglen, managed to overcome all criticism because she was as chic as a fashion model. Her tennis clothes were beautiful and she holds a lacy cardigan—or shawl, perhaps—and a dear little bag encircled by a floral band. It is a far cry from the huge holdall modern lady champions carry to court.

Golf, tennis, and tanning on the beach became fashionable pastimes. For women, the playing of games or indulgence in physical exercise were truly liberating, declarations that they were not to be hidden in modest clothes or enfeebled by lack of muscular activity.

BELOW: The keen interest in sport, particularly tennis, among the upper classes, is expressed in this vanity case. Now, this would be a well-chosen gift for a beloved and keen tennis partner. It is made of molded plastic. The vanity case is in the collection of the Museum of Fashion, Bath, England.

Tiffany & Co

LEFT: The famous trademark blue shopping bag promises to deliver a wonderful gift, whether jewelery or an exquisite vanity case.

BELOW: The Tiffany premises on Broadway, where the shop opened as a "fancy goods emporium" in the early ninteenth century. The company acquired silver, glass, and leather workshops where they employed hundreds of craftsmen, retailing the products through the store.

In 1837, Charles Tiffany opened a store selling bric-a-brac at 259 Broadway, New York. He realized it would be profitable to employ his own craftsmen and opened studios producing fine jewelery.

Tiffany believed machinery was an aid to the craftsman and, because he mixed the machine-made with the handmade, he was able to keep ahead of his competitors.

After the First World War, the Tiffany company spotted a market for metal clutches, cigarette cases, lighters, lipstick cases, and powder compacts, and seized the opportunity to create these items as jewelery. Tiffany products became a high status symbol during the 1920s, a reputation they have maintained ever since.

The company no longer belongs to the Tiffany family and now has retail outlets all over the world. Tiffany has become one of the world's most famous jewelers, and continues to create luxury clasps, handbags, and purses.

LEFT: Use the name "Tiffany" in song or literature and, instantly, the world sees glamour and luxury. One of the world's most famous jewelers and luxury goods stores, Tiffany & Co inhabit a suitably grand building in New York City.

The leather makers, particularly Hermès and Vuitton, emerged as major manufacturers of fine leather handbags designed to meet these new feminine demands. The sturdy Bolide from Hermès appeared in 1923; it was simple in shape and elegantly short of ornamentation, and was exactly suited to the young woman zooming, in her smart little racer, from the exercise gymnasium to the golf club.

LEFT: This ring-meshed bag makes a quirky use of color, inspired no doubt by the then-radical paintings from contemporary artists. Also, by this time synthetic dyes supplied a range of colors not possible with natural dye. The metal mount holds the fabric firm, and the thin chain handle is designed to dangle from the arm.

BELOW: Designers adapted the Japanese inro, used to carry herbs, into a vanity case for cosmetics. Sometimes, tassels hid an extra fitting to hold lipstick. The vanity cases came in ivory, precious metals, or synthetic materials. Faux ivory was popular. Here, the carved image pays homage to a common Japanese motif, the chrysanthemum. The Museum of Fashion in Bath owns this vanity case.

The 1920s saw a class of outrageously rich American and English industrialists whose beautiful wives and mistresses were well-known society figures, and they mixed freely with artists, poets, and cabaret entertainers. The changing society was revealed in the easy mix of aristocrats and showbiz personalities such as Lady Asher, Mrs Cole Porter, Nancy Cunard, Clara Bow, Pola Negri, and Lady Mountbatten. These rich women spent their time in hot pursuit of fashion, and their daring clothes and exploits entertained a weary public embittered by the dreadful war. These fashionable and extravagant women were constantly in the public eye because of photography and picture magazines, both products of this modern, inventive world.

LEFT: Lady Mountbatten, the wife of Lord Mountbatten, was renowned for her beauty and her wayward manners. She was famous, too, for her fashion sense and here she carries a superbly handcrafted leather handbag, an expensive and enviable possession.

ABOVE: The design of the mount is closer to pre-war motifs than those of the '20s. The arched center holds a complex setting of gems and intricately worked metal. This precious evening bag is part of the collection at the Museum of Fashion, Bath, England.

RIGHT: This intricately crafted evening bag is as decorative as a piece of jewelry. Even the chain handle is threaded with beads. The dark fabric of the pleated pouch serves as a foil to the complex ornament of the mount and clasp.

LEFT: During the '20s, the development of Cubism and abstract art influenced all aspects of design. This robust everyday handbag has been given a clever, and for its time, unexpected pattern of geometric shapes and lines. Colored leather insets and stitching enhance the design. The handles are stitched on and there is a zip closure, a new invention.

The "Bright Young Things," as the young rich were known, had time, plus money, and wildness and excess colored their post-war pleasures. And the women's handbags were expensive, simple, and exquisitely decorated with geometric designs. When money allowed, other women imitated the style, relying on the new synthetic fabrics to provide copies of the glamourous originals.

1930s
THRIFT AND INNOVATION

The Wall Street Crash of 1929 crumpled the chic world of the Bright Young Things. Their rich husbands and lovers were bankrupted overnight as stocks and shares tumbled across the industrial world, while millions of workers found themselves unemployed. Of course, a core of the very rich remained untouched, but the couture workshops of Paris indicated how small this group had become.

Georgina Howell, in her history of *Vogue* magazine, reports that "Chanel, who had one of the most expensive salons, cut her prices by half." Also, no American buyers visited the French fashion shows between 1929 and 1933, and designers used to displaying four hundred outfits at these events could now afford to produce only a hundred. Attitudes regarding displays of wealth hardened, and silly beauties with extravagant style were no longer admired.

RIGHT: Despite economic hardship, women did not abandon fashion altogether, and dress continued to be formal. Attending the races, these Englishwomen are correct in their hats and gloves, and all are carrying large clutches, in a variety of fabrics, including plastic.

HANDBAGS

In the early 1930s, the editors of *Vogue* took little notice of the change. The magazine continued to photograph rich, beautiful women. Fashion writers followed the American socialite, Mrs Wallis Simpson, admired for her immaculate chic, and Mrs Bryan Guinness (Diana Mitford, Lord Redesdale's daughter) was presented as an English beauty with wonderful style. Meanwhile, Lady Honor Channon posed in her elegant rococo dining salon.

Of course, poorer women retained their interest in fashion and, fortunately for them, factories came to the rescue. Shortages of silk and linen were met by further research into synthetic fabrics. Rayon was replaced by American nylon. Artificial silk and easy-to-wash cottons gave thousands access to inexpensive clothing, while plastic was no longer a firm, molded fabric but had evolved into a malleable material. Many consumer handbags were constructed from these new synthetic fabrics.

RIGHT: Barbara Stanwyk was one of the Hollywood glamour girls largely ignored by English fashion magazines. Her saucy expression under a jaunty hat, and her large, bossy handbag were a far cry from the haughty aristocratic beauties the fashionistas preferred, but the majority of women longed to emulate the Hollywood style.

LEFT: The clutch remained popular. This embroidered version, intended for evening wear, is enhanced by the use of metallic thread. It was made in India for the European market.

Plastic could be made to look like leather, tortoiseshell, ivory, or bone. It came in bright, clear colors; it could be gathered and pouched; and there was colorless, transparent plastic, which offered a previously unthinkable design potential.

The art world metamorphosed from intellectual Cubism to the fantastical work of the Dadaists and the Surrealists. The Surrealist photographer Man Ray specialized in unexpected views and lighting effects, while Salvador Dali painted scenes of the subconscious. These extraordinary, daring works inspired the designer Elsa Schiaparelli.

Her combinations of purples, pinks, and greens were radical; one sharp color even became known as "Schiaparelli pink." Her ideas were original and witty: she fashioned a handbag shaped as a seashell and another like a music box which tinkled noisily when it was opened. Her Lanterne was a rectangular handbag with a metal mount, but the interior was embossed with Dali line drawings and fitted with a mirror lit by electric bulbs whenever the handbag was opened.

LEFT: Designers were intrigued by the potential of synthetic fabrics. This handbag uses Alumesh to create an unusual surface. It was designed for Whiting and Davis, the American department store.

Chanel

Gabrielle Bonheur Chanel (1883–1971), known as Coco, was born in a poorhouse and trained as a seamstress. With financial help from lovers, she opened shops in Brittany and—in 1920—in Paris. She designed for active, elegant women and her bags were to become classic best sellers. Her output was enormous, but in 1939 she closed her couture department, keeping only the production of accessories and perfumes. In the 1940s she was threatened with legal action for supposed pro-Nazi activities. The French rejected her work though the American and British markets were not affected. She resumed clothing design only in 1954. Her heirs are the sons of a former Chanel partner. They own the House of Chanel, while Luxottica group run the company. The brilliant Karl Lagerfeld is the chief designer and his work has made Chanel a huge company, a worldwide leader in the high-end market for handbags, clothes and perfume.

LEFT: Chanel's headquarters are housed in this grand building in Paris, France. It is the heart of a huge commercial operation, a major leader in global high fashion and accessories.

RIGHT: Coco Chanel is wearing her own classic wardrobe. She adored and promoted ropes of pearls as an accessory, and the jacket of her famous suit is invariably piped along the edges and collar—as it is here. She was a successful businesswoman as well as an original fashion designer.

LEFT: Chanel had a knack of creating timeless pieces. Her quilted handbag with chain handles has survived in its basic form, although it has gone through many variations. This version has a curved edge on the closing flap but it still carries her famous logo.

RIGHT: Displayed in the window of a Chanel shop in Venice in 2009, is a variation on the classic Chanel jacket and versions of her quilted bag.

HANDBAGS

BELOW: The silver metal mount and the decorative stitching on this purple bag make subtle reference to the contemporary Art Deco style of sleek, geometric pattern.

RIGHT: Fashion in the '30s had fun breaking down old conventions. Purses did not have to be oblong or pouched, but could assume all sorts of interesting shapes. The model holds a firm triangular handbag with a metal "bangle" handle. Both design elements were a novelty.

Schiaparelli liked Rhodophane, a new plastic, and with it she made a transparent purse. It was fun, but it broke a cardinal handbag rule: it exposed the secret, interior world of a woman's life. Unlike other couture houses, Schiaparelli mass-produced handbags, but no matter how outrageous in design, her handbags were functional and comfortable to use. Others imitated her daring, though with much less panache. There were handbags shaped like passenger liners or automobiles, and doggy-shapes were also marketed. All these, though, were passing fancies.

LEFT: "Simplicity is the keynote of true elegance" was a favorite saying of Coco Chanel. Her idea is proved true in this thin, smooth-surfaced handbag, decorated with a single simple jewel. This bag is part of the Lady Mattheson Collection in the Bath Museum, England.

Workingwomen preferred sensible handbags to serve their day-to-day needs. The classic designers led the way. Hermès made a simple, capacious handbag called Plume; it carried little ornament, closed with a zipper and had short double handles attached to unobtrusive gilt links.

A year earlier, in 1932, Vuitton had presented the Noe bag, an elegant variation of the old workbag, though Vuitton based his design on a horse feedbag. Its large, leather pouch was closed by a leather drawstring but was carried by separate leather straps buckled together. The length could be adjusted. Mass market manufacturers used plastic and nylon for cheaper versions.

RIGHT: This fabric handbag, designed for everyday use, has a complex corded surface creating a wonderful texture. It came from a manufacturer called Normandie.

The fashionable wooed European art and artists, but the greatest fashion influence came from the United States where Art Deco swept away the minimalism of the 1920s. Art Deco is at its best as architectural ornament, but the "zigzags and dense floral fields, faceted crystalline forms, stripings of various sorts"—as the architectural historian Spiro Kostof described them—were suited just as well to jewelry and handbags. Jewelers decorated purses with Art Deco motifs, fashioned from gold, gems. and semi-precious stones.

LEFT: Designs during the '30s tended towards bold pattern and color. Dull metallic chain handles and mount offset the daring stripes on this handbag.

For much of the decade, *haute couture* designers ignored the influence of Hollywood on the popular imagination. They were disdainful of film actresses and underestimated the glamour of the movies. Even Chanel was not successful when she was employed in Hollywood. Her narrow silhouette in muted, tasteful colors, so adored in Europe, looked merely drab on film. Instead, the flamboyant Schiaparelli was more successful, creating costumes for screen divas Mae West and Zsa Zsa Gabor.

Hollywood films showed confident, self-sufficient women in office outfits or wearing pleated skirts and shorts—but all swinging functional handbags. Joan Crawford, Marlene Dietrich, and Tallulah Bankhead gave a vision of independent womanhood, hair loose and waved, clothing tailored but feminine and smart. The majority of women loved these glamorous images and longed to imitate them.

ABOVE: This slinky satin clutch uses purple cleverly contrasted with side insets of pink. While the Art Deco diamante clasp adds an extra dash of evening glamour.

BELOW: This velvet evening bag has an unexpected, divided flap, joined by a glittering closure. The luxury fabric and the sparkling Art Deco clasp enrich the simplicity of the design.

Schiaparelli

Elsa Schiaparelli (1890-1973) was brought up in an intellectual, noble Roman family, and in her youth sought the company of painters and writers. When her husband deserted her and their baby daughter, she made and sold hats for a living. Unlike Chanel, she was not driven by ambition, but enjoyed the whimsical aspects of fashion. In 1929 she opened a shop in Paris. Though she was not an artist, she was bursting with ideas, and she persuaded her artist friends such as Giacometti and Man Ray to interpret her creativity. Her fabrics were painted with lobsters, while her bags assumed strange shapes and unexpected color. Shiaparelli also made perfumes.

She spent World War II in New York, but later returned to Paris. However, the post-war society of a ruined and desolate Europe did not respond to her eccentric, comic designs; the prevailing mood was too somber. Shiaparelli closed her design house in 1954, though her reputation as a designer has only strengthened with the years.

LEFT: Whiting and Davis, a well known department store in New York, was sure that its customers knew the famous Parisian designer Schiaparelli because she had worked in the American city as a young woman. Their Christmas advertisement in the 1937 November issue of American *Vogue* proudly announced handbags designed in the "Schiaparelli style."

ABOVE: Her shop, photographed in the 1940s in the Place Vendôme, Paris, shows very feminine window dressing behind a model in a severe suit, a scooped Schiaparelli hat, and carrying a clutch of interesting shape on a metal mount.

They liked the movie clothes of suits and shirtdresses, the robust handbags, large pouches on squared-off mounts or roomy, firm rectangles. In the evening the stars carried clutches, now a softer version than the sharp rectangle of the 1920s. Chrome, Vitrolite glass, and glossy plastics were put to good use.

The department stores sold handbags and clutches with striped surfaces or carrying an ornament of zigzags, and gave them plastic "bangle" handles. Art Deco could be found everywhere in unusual handle arrangements, with big metal circles linked onto chain handles. The higher end of the market employed shell and animal horn, although these natural materials were quite expensive. There were still shoppers, however, who could afford the status of the natural, if not the precious.

RIGHT: The designers of the 1920s were endlessly imaginative. This clutch sports an unusual, tiered mount that displays the beautiful markings of snakeskin.

LEFT: Semi-circles in stitched ribbing are set in an asymmetrical pattern against the metal semicircles of the handle, and this creates a clever, interesting effect on this daywear suede purse.

RIGHT: It is no surprise that every woman regards her handbag as private territory. This is where she stores many small and vital components of life: keys, hairpins, photographs, lipstick, perfume, and the like. They convey sentiment, necessity, and intimacy, and are too personal to suffer scrutiny. Mostly, these items were not tidily arranged, although '30s vanity cases with discrete interior pockets were intended to promote a neat filing system: not always successfully.

The world of high fashion did catch up. In 1939 Schiaparelli made a copy of a postman's bag, worn over the shoulder. Elizabeth Arden, the cosmetics entrepreneur, created vanity cases fully fitted with bottles, manicure sets, and brushes, designed for air and rail travel. These cases were, in appearance, similar to a small hatbox and the double handle was fashioned from firm, short straps centered on the lid. In Rome an unknown craftsman named Fendi began to make hand-stitched handbags in dignified designs that brought the rich to his door.

LEFT: This unusual barrel-shaped bag and the criss-crossed cord covering its surface coordinate with the pleating of the model's dress. This handbag, stylish and roomy, is another example of the ingenuity of the bag makers of this decade.

Fendi

This brand is associated with baroque decoration and superb craftsmanship, yet when Edoardo and Adele Fendi opened in Rome in 1925 they concentrated on conservative, but beautifully made travel bags and handbags. They did not keep up with modernity, instead relying on classic designs, but in the 1960s they employed an unknown German designer, Karl Lagerfeld, to bring a little zip to the company. He persuaded them into the ready-to-wear market. When Sylvia Fendi took over as design co-ordinator in 1992, she brought an equally dynamic approach. Her handbags were romantic and bohemian, and women yearned to own her Baguette.

Fendi remains in family hands and has branched out into the production of jeans, glasses, pens, and menswear. A synthetic waterproof fabric produced by its researchers boosted sales considerably. Fendi now has outlets in Europe, the USA, and Japan, and its handbags are prized for their quality and interesting design.

LEFT: Fendi is recognized for its sleek presentation and the modernity of its store fronts, yet the interiors are relaxed with the atmosphere of a grand bazaar.

RIGHT: The Silvia Fendi influence is displayed on the shelves where an array of extraordinary handbags can be seen. Here are dyed furs, gorgeous colors, embroideries, baubles, and a handbag that is a bold mix of fur and leather. Fendi manufactures a variety of clothes, handbags, shoes, sunglasses, and associated products. Some of these, such as versions of the popular Baguette handbag, come in limited editions of high workmanship

BELOW: Silvia Venturini Fendi has been instrumental in moving the family workshop into modernity. As a designer she is inspired by rich fabrics, eccentric ornaments, and the originality of hippie style.

HANDBAGS

Vogue began to feature movie stars and write about their clothes and make-up. In recognition of leaner economic times, the magazine even gave dressmaking advice and published paper dress patterns. Elsewhere, Chanel and other designers moved into making cotton, pique, faux silk, and nylon acceptable to the couture world.

The larger world, though, was an uneasy place. From 1936 to 1939 Spain endured a vicious civil war, and idealists came from across the world to support one side or the other. The Fascist dictators, Hitler and Mussolini, moved into positions of power. Across Europe marching men in strange uniforms demonstrated the frightening politics of totalitarian Fascism.

RIGHT: The old, complex craft of the leather worker was not forgotten despite the influx of synthetic materials. This blue leather handbag is skilfully stitched to form a swirling pattern across the surface. The handle is attached to links, then threaded through rings to ensure a firm hold.

High society was not so admirable: Diana Mitford, by this time no longer Mrs Guinness, was in love with the British Fascist leader, Oswald Mosley, who became her second husband. And *Vogue* may have enjoyed relating the scandal of Mrs Wallis Simpson and her marriage to the King, as well as the bombshell of his abdication, but no longer did these high society figures arouse the public's admiration. Now even haughty fashion writers conceded that film stars were infinitely preferable to these dubious aristocrats.

LEFT: As the decade closed, women turned to large purses but they did not always favor the trend for a bag of military design. This handbag has a feminine cut, its gently curved flap enhanced by a flat bow and glass beads.

Women's clothes started to carry a hint of military style. Dark colors were prominent, while epaulettes and brass buttons trimmed coats and suit jackets. Handbags, too, assumed a brisk utilitarian look, albeit with a touch of luxe But decoration grew subdued and discreet as the all-important purse grew large and sensible with strong, almost masculine clasps.

The movie comedian, Groucho Marx, described the decade as the "Threadbare Thirties" because modest clothing and handbags with a distinctly plain, sensible air challenged the cheeky glitz of the 1920s. And as war approached, fashion became sombre: the traits of frivolity and constant, careless change, were now hard to justify.

LEFT: The affection for the traditional decoration of needlework in a floral design has never disappeared, whatever the fashion. This handbag was crafted in Austria and was destined for the quality market.

LEFT: As the '30s ended, increased military activity caused a shortage of leather, so instead reptile skins were used more frequently in handbag manufacture. This sturdy clutch has little adornment but the markings of the skin compensate for this.

1940s
MARCHING ORDERS

The cute military touches favored by the designers of the late 1930s grew into serious army uniforms with the declaration of war in 1939. Women joined the services and found themselves in regulation gear. However, they preferred not to carry any military touches on their civilian clothes.

In Great Britain, the government placed restrictions on the fashion industry. Clothes rationing coupons were introduced in 1941, and the Making of Clothes (Restrictions) Orders arrived in 1942. The fashion world was further affronted by the Utility Restrictions. This ordered that two-thirds of clothes coupons had to be used on government Utility clothes. Even the wealthy were affected by this, and "Make-do-and-mend" became the battle cry.

LEFT: Army girls wear smart, starchy uniforms and seem delighted by the fashion show presenting government Utility dresses. These were commissioned by the state and the haut couturist, Norman Hartnell, supplied some of the designs. The shoes, snazzy high heels and even a pair of strappy delights, must have excited the audience who, by contrast, were wearing stout, sensible, low-heeled shoes. But only one Utility model carries a handbag; a large clutch. Wartime shortages of materials caused difficulties in the manufacture of this all-important accessory. Besides, handbags were not given the respect due to them; even fashion photographs tended to neglect them.

Wartime women took to handiwork; antique fabrics were stretched over worn-out handbags, or the bag was cut away and the replacement fabric attached to the mount. Women knitted and crocheted pouches to fit on the mounts, and knotted string bags on drawstrings were made. Old-fashioned linen or cotton workbags, replete with a little light embroidery, also made an appearance.

BELOW: Housewives resorted to string bags of macramé or they crocheted wool to make workbags. Manufacturers too were forced to consider these alternative materials. A French manufacturer used a thick wool and crocheted this very pleasing triangular pouch onto which a clear plastic bangle handle was attached.

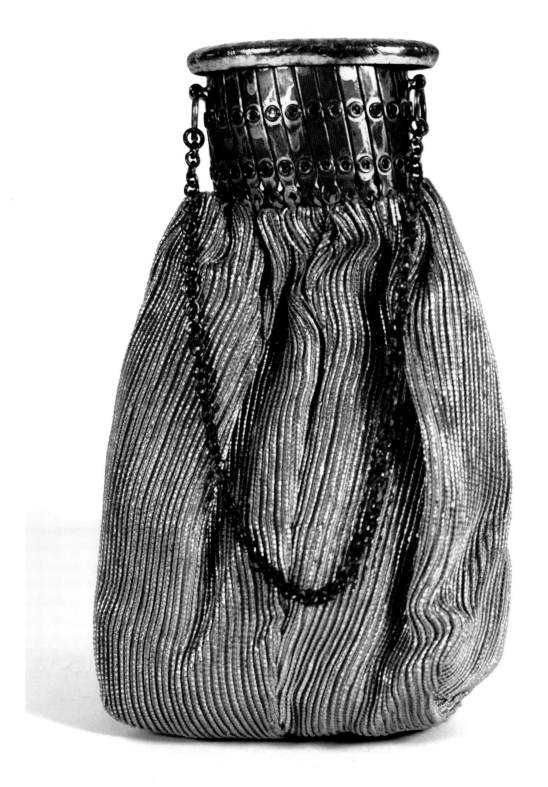

It had become difficult for women to look fragile and helpless. Women were working as bus conductors and errand boys, in munitions factories and on farms. Textiles were in short supply and clothes inevitably assumed a clumsy cut with boxy jackets, pants, and plain suits. In the fashion photographs of Norman Parkinson, his 1941 models carry firm, rectangular bags carried on double handles. Nevertheless, as the war continued, the handbag changed.

LEFT: Smart women, and no doubt a few factory owners, re-used metal mounts from old bags. Clever little concertina closures, associated with pre-war metal mesh purses, appeared with pouches made of gold lamé fabrics to create glitzy evening bags. Despite the war, couples still enjoyed a night out at a dinner-dance nightclub and what self-respecting gal wanted to haul a huge sensible handbag round with her!

BELOW: A concertina closure is inherently decorative because, when it is closed, the metal rods fold to form a textured surface, catching light and shadow. This kind of closure is an interesting variation on the drawstrings that, traditionally, are used to open and close a small, gathered pouch.

Koret

Richard Koret and Henry Gould opened their design house in New York in 1929. Their business was the design, manufacture, and distribution of handbags. Naming the company Koret, they were innovative in their approach, eager to experiment with new synthetic materials. Although not craftsmen in the old European sense, they had a strong sense of design and were determined to make synthetics pleasing to the top end of the market. The company developed a soft, slurred surface to plastic fabrics, and invented Koretolope, a faux suede. Koret became a leading style authority. Its Doctor's Bag was very popular and Jackie Kennedy Onassis favored its products. Koret formed associations with Christian Dior and Givenchy, major *haute couture* designers. Then the company became involved in a long copyright battle with a Californian company that used the name Koret; the Californians now makes clothes only, while Koret continues to manufacture handbags

RIGHT: This company responded to the novelty of plastics, but did not deviate from classic design as demonstrated in this faux black patent leather handbag.

RIGHT: This sleek handbag is given a luxury note with a beautifully worked metal clasp. During this decade, people were not dismissive of synthetics, a snobbery that came into fashion much later.

ABOVE: Koret followed the leather workers' tradition and finished their synthetic Koretolope products with meticulous interiors, proudly labeled and bearing the company logo.

Women were also doing physical work. They cycled, baled straw, drove tractors, and worked as street cleaners. Hands needed to be free to work, but no woman was going to abandon her purse. Women looked for straps that fitted across their chests or hung from their shoulders. Bags designed to fit on belts made an appearance. Schiaparelli's 1939 postman's bag hanging off the shoulder was copied, while the big rectangular purse was given long straps to hook over the shoulder. Leather and metals, zippers, and clasps were scarce in wartime.

LEFT: The long shoulder straps on one of the bags may be something of a novelty to this young shopper, but this style was popular after Schiaparelli introduced it in Paris. The other bag has a short thick handle to hang on the wrist. The bags shown here were designed by Norman Hartnell, and both are spacious, sturdy bags, suited to demanding, unpredictable war conditions.

BELOW: As more and more men were called to the army, women filled civilian jobs. The authorities were wise enough to supply feminine, utilitarian handbags for their new intake of bus conductors. The bus company have adapted the Schiaparelli look with handbags slung across the chest.

CATERHAM
GODSTONE
REDHILL

JEYES' FL
THE BEST DISINFECTANT AND

Wartime designers were inhibited, and they could not turn to artists to inform their work because the war absorbed the energies of painters and photographers. They were called to make documentaries or record battles in paint or photography. Some disappeared to the safety of the USA. Writers tended to be pessimistic, or wrote escapist adventure tales. But entertainment did not stop, and there were long queues at theaters and movie houses.

British actresses provided a glimpse of glamour: Ann Todd sported a little pillbox hat of velvet and net, while Vivien Leigh matched a tweed jacket with a print dress. Deborah Kerr, meantime, trimmed black outfits with a dash of color. Fabrics were swathed round the body, tiny pleats being tucked into seams as a contrast to the practical look of Utility gear. But it was American movie stars who enthralled women everywhere. The crimson lipstick of the still-popular Joan Crawford, her mannish but not masculine suits, her high heels, and her handbags were closely imitated. Betty Grable and Rita Hayworth, with their flowing hair, slinky dresses and long slit skirts, were much admired.

RIGHT: This handbag is made from grosgrain although the designer has folded and pulled the fabric as if it were leather. The color and the rhinestone ornament mark this as a formal, even an evening bag, but its size and shape mean it would prove a useful day bag too.

LEFT: Deborah Kerr was adored as an actress, but she did not represent the obvious face of glamour. Her refined beauty is offset here by the luxury of velvet and lace. Her purse is classic, a conventional design in the wartime material of reptile skin.

BELOW: A clutch that makes no pretence to simulate leather, but positively revels in using silk bearing an unusual contemporary stamped pattern. The closure makes charming use of a colored plastic clasp.

In France, the couture houses faced restrictions from the German occupiers, but these did not seem as severe as the British regulations.

Designers such as Balenciaga and Paquin took note of the homemakers' bags and translated the make-do designs into brocade and satin "reticules" with braiding and tassels. Crochet was made big, chunky and interesting, and manufacturers turned to synthetic fabrics.

ABOVE: Interiors were more demanding but the new plastics did not yet fold as easily as leather. The designer here has included an interior purse on a spindle.

RIGHT: Manufacturers and designers were determined to make the best use of synthetics. This handbag has an elegant Art Deco style trim, stitched with quiet little triangles and its plastic clasp is elegant, even luxurious in appearance. The whole thing looks neither cheap nor synthetic.

War research had, of course, refined these materials. Schiaparelli made a handbag from rayon printed with a pattern of ration tickets, and canvas bags like military knapsacks came onto the market. Anne Marie of France made quirky bags to defy the gloomy war atmosphere, while the American designer Koret was inventive in his use of imitation tortoiseshell, plastics, and corduroy. One bag had a giant safety pin as its handle, a witty reference to wartime security. The department stores carried small stocks of plastic pouches, faux postman bags, and ingeniously elegant handbags.

Gucci

BELOW: Gucci gained early fame for expanding the use of material beyond leather, and its creative use of canvas has always been appreciated. The bag has all the traits of a Gucci classic, and the labeled linen bag is given to customers to protect their Gucci purchase.

Guccio Gucci (1869–1953) and his family opened a leather shop in Florence in 1927. They were proud of their craftsmanship and gained a reputation for high quality. However, they could not avoid the problem of shortages in materials during World War II. Undeterred, the company made handbags with bamboo handles. By the 1960s it had outlets in the Far East and, until the 1970s, maintained its superior market position. Unfortunately, the Gucci family were volatile and quarrelsome, traits that badly affected the business. After lawsuits and even a prison sentence for one Gucci man, the family accepted a major shake-up in the company. In 1989 the designers Geoffrey Beene and Calvin Klein were hired, but it was Tom Ford, appointed creative director in 1993, who restored the reputation of Gucci. Gucci is now owned by Pinault-Printemps-Redoute, and holds its position as a prime fashion house.

LEFT: This vibrant window display reflects the modernity of today's Gucci company. The color and energy on show belies the high quality of the company's products.

Designers and manufacturers were forced to find ways to close handbags without metal clasps or zippers. Wood and bamboo were tried as mounts, loops and buttons, and toggles substituted for clasps. Large, flat envelope bags, the flap closed with a loop and button, were favored, and the same method of closing was applied to the flaps of big shoulder bags.

RIGHT: This handbag has avoided all use of metal. A simple envelope of deerskin, a material that could be found locally in the UK and parts of the USA and, in the way utilized here, not requiring sophisticated treatment. But this handbag is elevated to simple elegance through the design of the handle, a semi-circle of clear plastic bound with cord of the same fabric as the handbag.

Handles secured by gilt links were replaced by a loop stitched to the bag. This was either long enough to twist round the wrist, or short enough to fit snugly on it. Parkinson shows a 1941 model with a tiny bag held on a thick handle fitted round her wrist. These loops were made of the same fabric as the handbag.

LEFT: A faux crocodile skin pouch has been bunched into an angular plastic mount. This has deep sides and is squared-off. The design and materials create an interesting, stylish handbag.

BELOW: The handles are cleverly knotted through holes drilled in the mount, thus eliminating gilt links or, indeed, any use of metal. It is a triumph of design using the comparatively new synthetic plastic.

In Paris most couture houses closed: (many of their owners were anyway exiles in New York.) and French *Vogue* was banned. This gave British designers a chance, and Norman Hartnell, Worth, Hardy Amies, and Angéle Delanghe established themselves in the fashion world. Department stores in London did their best to supply stylish clothes for their customers. They knew, as did the writers at *Vogue*, that women wanted to look good for their men when they returned from the Front.

Factories, although restricted, kept dress and handbag sales alive and did their best with coupons and Utility clothes. John Lewis moved their fitting rooms to bomb shelters, while Dickens & Jones provided tea for weary clients. Suits and dresses which were permitted only a few yards per garment as decreed by government, were necessarily severe but ingenious women had ways to soften the look.

RIGHT: Designers had fun looking for alternative materials and sometimes this meant any traditional sense of handbag design and color was blown away. This delightfully gaudy vanity bag relies on metal fittings but the fabric is coiled telephone wires. Telephones in the '40s were attached to a dialling box with long tightly coiled plastic covered wires, and didn't they make an excellent handbag fabric?

LEFT: This handbag seems to have been constructed from off-cuts of suede and leather found in the workshop. The clasp is a neat shell-shaped plastic, and the whole effect is interesting and classy.

Selfridges

LEFT: Mr Harry Gordon Selfridge became a well known and respected public figure in London after the introduction of his innovative retail methods in the early twentieth century.

BELOW: Even in 2009 his department store continues to create a sense of shopping glamour as revealed in this photo, depicting the handbag department in Selfridges in London, England.

This famous London department store opened for business in 1909. The owner, H. Gordon Selfridge (1858–1947), came from the USA and was determined to introduce the concept of the American department store to Londoners. These stores were a logical response to mass-production. Craftsmen were reluctant to lower their prices, yet shoppers wanted cheap goods. In the department store they were offered a wide range of products. During the two world wars, particularly, shoppers in the department store were certain they would find, despite shortages, a choice of handbags. Today Selfridges is an outlet for both crafted and factory products. The shop has changed hands a few times but is now owned by Galen Weston. In the early twenty-first century it underwent a major refurbishment under the design direction of Paul Kelly. Its handbag department definately caters for the luxury market.

LEFT: The designer, Louis Tiffany said railroad stations should be as grand as palaces, and certainly the neo-classical Selfridges building offered majesty to everyone. The owner wanted shoppers to feel awe and pleasure when they encountered his department store in London and the vast crowds who visited the splendid new store proved his ambitions were not wrong.

In France, Schiaparelli enhanced close-fitting black suits with arrows embroidered in her famous pink. The Italian designer Balenciaga inserted gathered yokes on the shoulders and hips of a dress; the dress was black but the yokes were violet. Home dressmakers imitated this by re-cycling old dresses to renew their outfits. Skirts and blouses proved a cunning way to overcome fabric shortages, while beading and embroidery broke the monotony of plain fabrics.

There was little sign of these alternative decorations on homemade handbags. Knitting and crochet work could be carried about but they were things to do on the bus or sitting in the underground, which was not possible with the fiddle of embroidery threads, beads, or sequins. Instead in France, Great Britain, and the USA, knitted bead pouches appeared. These were bags decorated with plastic or natural beads stitched or glued in interesting geometric patterns.

LEFT: This is the most beautiful, subtle response to the shortage of leather during the war. Narrow bronze colored cords are closely laid, curved and twisted to form a pattern of rhythmic lines and texture. This is marked as a "genuine Cordé" product.

BELOW: The plastic clasp, in two tones, echoes the color of the cord, while the handles, held on plastic links, have also been made of closely stitched cord.

RIGHT: When World War II ended, the Americans set in motion the Marshall Plan, an economic scheme to revitalize a ruined, bombed out Europe. To their delight, German women found their shops filled with lovely plastic American purses, soft and luxurious, in a wondrous range of pastel colors. Technical research for military purposes had spilled into the civilian area and the world of handbags had been vastly improved.

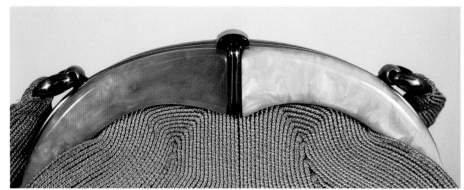

In the USA delightful plastic handbags were manufactured in pale blues, yellows, greens, and pinks. But in the fashion shots of British Utility wear, the models carry crocheted bags on long tapes slung over the shoulder or knotted string bags clutched in the hand. The Utility office tried to promote gas mask handbags, but *Vogue* never showed these clunky things and the public didn't take to them. Until the late 1940s, handbags remained huge and were fitted with inner compartments and purses. Plastic was used to experiment with trapezoids, beehives, and concertina shapes, the Americans being in the forefront of such development.

LEFT: There were sincere attempts to make the gas mask bag look like a charming, quirky purse. It was one of those little, lost battles of World War II. *Vogue* never bothered to present it, and who wanted to carry the clumsy thing? Besides, it was not a proper purse, handy for storing a girl's money, lipstick, comb, keys, and other important things? It mattered little that the essential mask, shown here, fits neatly into the handbag. This relic is part of the Museum of Fashion in Bath, England and looks as if it has never been used.

Then in Paris in 1947, Christian Dior presented his sensational New Look, consisting of long flared skirts, soft shoulders, and tiny waists. He banished masculine padded shoulders and large, functional handbags. Instead the latter had to be small and carried in the hand, as shoulder slings ruined the gentle shoulder line.

The war was over, and British women refused to be regulated any longer. Europe was enjoying American imports and in Great Britain, where clothes rationing continued, suppliers found themselves with piles of Utility clothes while their customers mysteriously flaunted extravagant skirts and—occasionally—a gorgeous plastic handbag from the USA.

ABOVE: Big clutches saw out the last of the '40s. The examples shown here are made of real leather; both are sumptuous and quietly luxurious. The red snakeskin is folded over and two metal strips form the mount. These are magnetic, and close together with a smart little click.

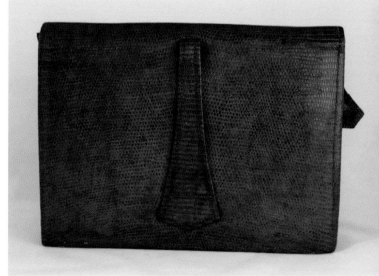

RIGHT: This golden brown snakeskin clutch is an envelope shape and has a fold over flap as a closure. This is the back view, showing the flat handle stitched on the surface. To hold the clutch, the wearer slips her hand through this handle rather than holding the handbag under her arm, clutching it against her body.

1950s
LADIES vs PIN-UPS

After World War II, the United States emerged as the world's leading nation. The British Empire began to crumble, and the Soviet Union menaced from behind its "Iron Curtain." The followers of high fashion, however, took little notice of these great events. They concentrated on Paris and *haute couture*.

Norman Parkinson photographed images of cool beauties in beautifully tailored clothes, carrying elegant handbags. Actually, it is a curious thing that in these and other fashion studies, handbags are rarely on display. The likely explanation is that the great houses, whose clothes were being photographed, gave little significance to handbag design.

LEFT: After World War II, an exhausted Europe turned admiring eyes towards the United States. The glamour of America was perceived through Hollywood films, and exuberant, gorgeous movie stars. Jayne Mansfield was Marilyn Monroe's chief competitor for the "blonde bombshell" tag. Here, Jayne and the starlet Natalie Wood, adorn a sports car at a drive-in restaurant. A close look reveals a vanity case on the floor of the automobile—a bag every young woman longed to own.

HANDBAGS

But this accessory did matter. In 1952 Chanel hit the headlines with her quilted bag, which was wide and narrow and carried on a chain handle. She named it the 2.55, the date she revealed it to an adoring public. Three years later, when she was pregnant by her husband Prince Rainier of Monaco, Grace Kelly carried a Hermès bag. It was instantly re-branded the Kelly bag, a covetable accessory even though it was a revival of an earlier product, a dignified purse with little ornament and an unobtrusive clasp. Elizabeth Arden, meantime, turned out fine vanity cases with cleverly organized interiors.

The fashion pages of the time give glimpses of structured handbags made of leather. Carried against a tweed outfit, crocodile or ostrich skin were favored, while patent, diamanté, metal, and brocades complemented a ball dress. Handbags and shoes matched each other in color and material, and the coordinated ensemble became the aim of the correct and sophisticated wardrobe.

RIGHT: The bag was one of the superbly crafted products from Hermès, known to an elite few until Grace Kelly, the movie-star-turned-princess, was photographed carrying one. The handbag was instantly named the Kelly, and continues to be a best seller.

LEFT: Each Hermès Kelly bag is handmade, and can be soft or, as shown, structured. The craftsman spends at least eighteen hours making one bag. The client chooses the leather they prefer, but the interior is always lined with goatskin. All the seams are stitched, then the leather waxed and polished. The last step is to stamp, in gold, the words "Hermès, Paris" on the finished bag.

Handbag decoration was subdued and saddle stitching quietly marked the leather. Nonetheless, there was a strange taste for handbags of reptile skins where the head and claws of the lizard provided dubious decoration. In France there was a handbag range in which the handles were a square or circular opening, cut into the upper section of the body, so becoming an extension of the bag itself.

LEFT: This handbag is unostentatious but luxurious. The gleaming black reptile skin needs no adornment and the mount is unobtrusive. In mood and design, it epitomizes the elegance of the '50s and was produced for the high end of the market.

LEFT: Vanity cases were to become a major teenage fad, but the fashionable versions were not like this dignified grown-up version, small, neat, and arranged to dangle off the wrist.

BELOW: The interior is designed to hold cosmetics and perfume bottles and there is a further smaller white purse, probably for money. It is part of the fashion collection in the Bath Museum, England.

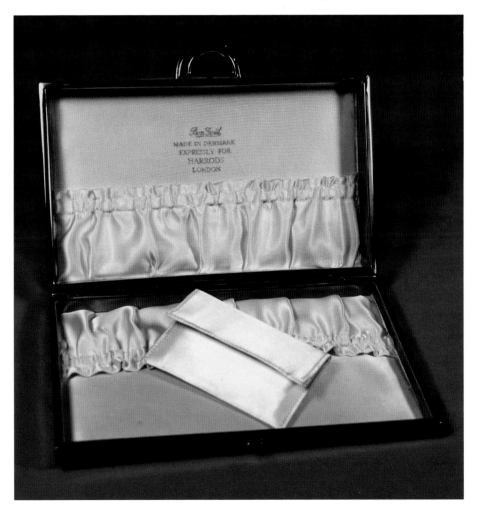

Wilardy

I n 1948 Will Hardy joined his father's company, Handbag Specialities, in Florida. He moved away from the metal favored by the company, and turned to plastic. Lucite was extremely tough with a rich, glossy appearance, but required hand molding and heat welding. Under the name Wilardy, he made handbags of unexpected shapes. Lucite allowed geometric cases with numerous facets, or boxes of swirled lines and curved silhouettes and popsicle handles. Hardy devised a concertina structure so the bag opened to reveal an interior of numerous layers. These were luxury products and when technology developed a machine method of molding and welding hard plastic, Wilardy bags lost out to mass production. The popular market was flooded with copies of his vanity cases which imitated his handles and pyramid shapes, and the original Wilardy Lucite handbags were relegated to the market for collectables.

RIGHT: The Wilardy cream Compact Bag has a mottled pearl surface adorned with rhinestones—all the characteristics admired by Koret fans. He gave it a hinged lipstick tube, easily found by the user and not at risk of rattling around the interior.

EXQUISITE Eiderdown calf bag has adjustable shoulder strap
and roomy outside pocket. Bag is separated into two compartments. Alongside is stunning ostrich pouch with single
handle. Theodore Rendl, 165 Madison Ave.

Over $25

EXTRA LARGE travel bag, a compact capacious
satchel by Lona Handbags, 136 Madison Ave.
Featured are two openings, one outside the other
concealed under the top frame. Both are roomy.

Have Large Roomy Bag Can Travel

A bag that travels must be large and roomy
with many pockets both inside and out.
All types of leathers are being shown for
resort and travel wear. Styling leans
toward the tailored look and colors know
no bounds. The shoulder strap is back!

PALOMINO fur gives a smart look to the tall bag at left
with a calf frame, tab and handle. At the right is a medium
size ostrich bag with a self-lock, covered frame and handle.
Walter Katten, 10 E. 33rd St.

LUCITE, a very important and attractive material. The box bag
at left is ornamented with jeweled names and a self-luggage-
handle; right is an oval shaped box with a jeweled lock and self-
handle. Wilardy, 347 Fifth Ave.

46

HANDBAGS & ACCESSORIES for December, 1959

ABOVE: This advertisement shows the wide range of designs made by
Wilardy, but he gained fame for his vanity cases. These were admired for
their unusual surfaces and designs. His designs for major fashion houses
moved his products into the top end of the market.

BELOW: Wilardy developed Lucite to be firm and smooth. His sturdy
Box Bag relies on a glossy Lucite surface and gilt clasp to give it's
geometric form a handsome appearance.

ABOVE: This very narrow design had a cleverly
designed interior with a mirror and elasticized
pockets. The woman using this had to confine her
intimate possessions to a neat filing system. This
rhinestone encrusted beauty was definitely for
evening use only.

In London, *Vogue* showed tailored suits and ball gowns with huge Cinderella skirts. Waists were tightly clinched, the bosom high and firm. Darts and diagonal seaming shaped the close-fitting Princess line. The image of women was of poised, corseted, well-groomed, creatures. There was a nod towards another world in the photographs of Anthony Armstrong-Jones. He captured models sprawled on deckchairs, spilling wine, or running towards a car, showing a world where women were carefree and imperfect.

Because there was another world and it was a very lively place: it was democratic, easygoing, and relaxed—and it was in the USA. The high-fashion writers, photographers, and mothers, too, hoped to persuade young women to be "ladylike," but an awful lot of girls had their eyes fixed on the movies. True, the *haute couture* crowd adored the movie actresses Audrey Hepburn and Ingrid Bergman, but then both women were essentially European, despite their Hollywood fame. And the American Grace Kelly fulfilled the dreams of the smart set when she married a European prince. Yet ordinary people saw another Hollywood. They preferred Mitzi Gaynor, Natalie Wood, and Marilyn Monroe.

LEFT: Fresh and youthful, Hollywood stars were fashion icons for young women everywhere. Wearing a wild polka dot frock, her hair clean but slightly tousled, the American actress, Mitzi Gaynor, attends the Cannes Film Festival in France in 1958. In her shiny-gloved hand, she carries a clutch. Her style was quite different from the carefully groomed, dignified couture presented by Paris at the time.

BELOW: These handbags were popularly known as vanity cases, and they were a far cry from the elegant style promoted by the *haut couture* houses in Paris. Vanity bags were invariably made from synthetic fabrics and came in jaunty patterns, such as this cheeky polka dot. Young girls loved the vanity cases.

RIGHT: Plastics were an exciting development, and both designers and shoppers were curious about the possibilities of the material. This vanity bag fully exploits the material. Made of Lucite, a molded, hard refinement invented by Will Hardy, the body is an interesting shape, and has an amusing flecked surface, never seen on leather.

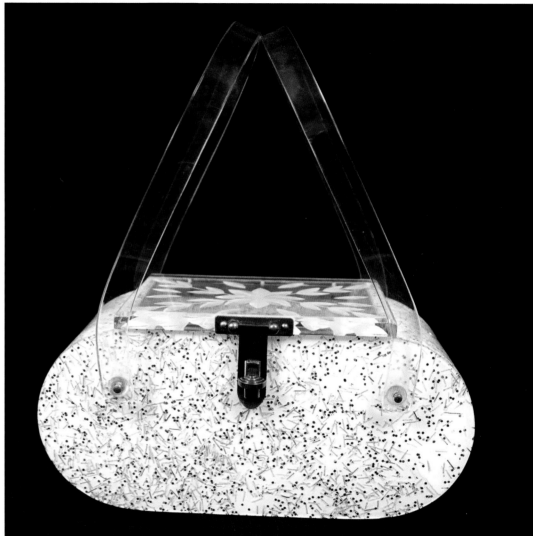

HANDBAGS

RIGHT: As plain as a lunch box in construction, the confetti pattern of the base, the etched lid, and the jeweled clasp contrive to create a charming vanity case. Part of the charm of the 1950s popular vanity cases was the fact that they were manufactured in a wide range of zany designs and patterns, all of great appeal to the young.

Young women yearned for peroxide blonde hair and the halter necks that Marilyn wore, and the permanently waved hair and pedal pushers of Mitzi. They wanted denim, frothy petticoats, striped, and polka-dotted nylon dresses. They wanted to look bright and informal. The arty crowd was excited by the tailoring of Teddy boys in England, but post-war girls preferred the rebel boys—Burt Lancaster, James Dean, and Marlon Brando in jeans, T-shirts, and cowboy boots.

BELOW: The extravagant decoration on this shopper handbag, all made in synthetic fabrics, may well have been labelled "kitsch" by the fashionistas. It expresses all the cheerful experimentation of the designers and manufacturers who were intrigued by the potential of plastics. The handbag epitomizes the uninhibited approach to dressing enjoyed by American women in the 1950s.

LEFT: This handbag uses shell set against silk and it has a bone handle, all natural products, perceived by some as superior to synthetic materials. However, the design comes from products originally made of colorful plastic tiles. Someone who felt free to experiment with his materials conceived the initial blueprint.

The designer, Claire McCardell, made ready-to-wear clothes that epitomized the American Look. She threw out the structured look and sold dresses that were comfortable to wear and easy to maintain. Enid Collins in far-away Texas made jaunty handbags in bright colors which were box-shaped vanity cases. These shapes with flat bases could sit safely on the car floor and could hold a change of nylons or a swimming costume. Before her marriage, Grace Kelly carried a capacious vanity bag in Alfred Hitchcock's *Rear Window*. Along with the usual items, she hid slippers and a negligee in this handbag.

LEFT: Initially, Lucite handbags were difficult to mold and expensive to produce, they sold to elite shoppers in Miami and Hollywood. The ridged, oval body has the appearance of highly polished wood and can be as sturdy.

ABOVE: The translucent lid etched for decoration, was very popular and so used frequently on Lucite vanity cases. Vanity bags were often deep enough to use as an overnight bag.

for the birds . . .

Enid Collins

LEFT: The various handiwork techniques used on this purse show Collins's extensive craft abilities. She has painted and beaded the artwork, but the wheels of the carriage are made with rolled-paper work. This is a Victorian craft, and involves cutting extremely narrow strips of stiff paper that are then folded into the shapes of leaves, swags, or the like. The shapes are glued to the surface. It is no wonder that her artistic handbags continue to carry great value.

BELOW: This shopping tote has been carefully constructed so that, despite its raffish air, it is in fact robust and sturdily put together. Collins stiffened fabrics to give them a firm structure but here, she has lined her edges and base with leather to ensure her bag can withstand daily use. The floral decoration is true to her love of free, colorful, illustration embellished with glass baubles and golden cord. Again, painting and glueing techniques have been used to make the decoration.

I n Texas, far removed from the iron hand of Parisian *haut couture*, Enid Collins and her sculptor husband, Frederick, took to making handbags on their ranch near Medina. Enid had studied fashion at the Texas Women's University and together, they prepared linen, leather, and papier mâché to mold stiff bucket shape totes and boxy vanity cases. Every bag was finished with leather interiors, mirrors, brass fittings, and clasps. The surfaces were hand-painted with whimsical illustrations of pineapples, shells, fishes, and birds, then adorned with glass and sequins. The decoration was free of elitism or tradition, and truly American in the novelty of its style. Enid Collins signed her bags and they carried her logo. The Tandy Leather Company bought the designs and logo but they ceased production in the '70s. Today, her handbags are highly valued by collectors of vintage purses.

BELOW: The interior of this vanity case bears Enid Collins's signature and the logo of the company she owned with her husband. As Texans, it was apt to choose a frolicking horse to identify their products. Her handbags were always signed.

LEFT: Enid Collins was more than a designer; she was also a skillful illustrator. This branch of lively birds is a delightful image and, as with all Collin's work, an unexpected motif to be found on a handbag.

The malleable quality and colors available in synthetics were fully exploited by American designers. Plastic was bent and patterned: a pink vanity case, for example, carried a transparent lid; floral sprays were etched into this lid, the marks shining against the pink surround, and circular handles, centered on the lid, were made of clear plastic. In addition, plastic flowers were applied to plastic surfaces and tiny plastic tiles in geometric rows ornamented big clutches.

In Florida, Jack de la Rose and Patricia of Miami created zany color mixes, guitar shapes, drum shapes, and irregular box shapes. Will Hardy used Lucite that, he claimed, would not yellow with age—a tendency in Bakelite and other synthetics. His rhinestone treasure chest was a status symbol, and his designs sold in Hollywood, Chicago, and New York. Will claimed that the curvaceous Marilyn Monroe had given him the initial inspiration.

LEFT: Italian women had turned to raffia and straw to make handbags during the shortages of the '40s. These proved popular with tourists and designers were quick to pick up the shoppers' enthusiasm. Plastic could be made to look like raffia, and this bag followed traditional handbag form—a far cry from the easy basket shapes of Italy—and imitated the raffia weave in sharp, unexpected color ways.

LEFT: Nylon and rayon proved good substitutes for cotton and silk. They, too, were hardy and washable and could be folded and pleated. This handbag exploits rayon silk, even twisting the fabric to create a novel clasp.

BELOW: This unusually flat design in patent leather reflects the sleek lines of 1950s American automobiles and household furniture. There are few other examples of this shallow shape, so perhaps handbag shoppers preferred their vanity case shape to be deep and spacious. However, this example is well used and the owner surely loved showing off her quirky design.

These styles did not stop in the USA but eventually traveled to Britain and Europe. Department stores everywhere stocked long clutches in faux patent or soft-textured plastics for those who were striving to imitate the elegant Parisian look. Craft workshops, such as Hermès and Vuitton, supplied the high end with natural leather and silks, but vanity cases in mock patent or plastic embossed to imitate straw and linen, were much appreciated by the popular market. The arts and crafts outlet, Liberty of London, offered clutches of machine-made broderie anglaise and floral prints. Few, though, could avoid the American influence. The Commonwealth that emerged from the old British Empire—Australia, Canada, and Africa— received American movies and products so attitudes there, too, were altered.

RIGHT: This shot of the smiling Hollywood star, Jean Peters, is a typical image of the carefree American teenage girl, with hair loose and bare feet. This vision encouraged girls all over the world to abandon the stuffy formalities taught them by their parents and prepared the way for the rebellions of western youth in the 1960s.

Elizabeth
Arden

Famous for beauty products, Elizabeth Arden (1878–1966) did not confine her work to one speciality. A Canadian, she studied in Paris before opening her own cosmetic company. In the 1930s, make-up was dismissed as an artificial horror for actresses, but Arden delighted women when she made lipstick to improve the look of an army outfit. She was among the first to make vanity cases a woman was proud to carry. In appearance a clutch or slightly pouched handbag on a square mount, these cases were "like a portable powder room for modern women on the hop." She used antelope or crocodile skins in elegant designs, or metal cases adorned with jewel-like decoration. Charles Jourdan and Oscar de la Renta were employed as her designers and to this day, the company retails cosmetic cases. Fabergé has owned Elizabeth Arden since 1988.

LEFT: Elizabeth Arden was a famous beautician, but her other love was horses. Her stables were a major force in American Thoroughbred racing and leading money winners. Notice the classy little tote she uses to carry sugar for her animals.

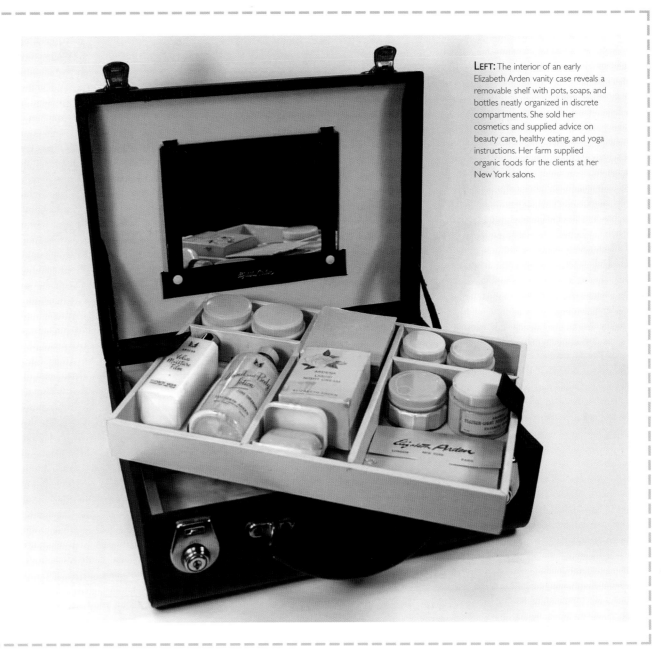

LEFT: The interior of an early Elizabeth Arden vanity case reveals a removable shelf with pots, soaps, and bottles neatly organized in discrete compartments. She sold her cosmetics and supplied advice on beauty care, healthy eating, and yoga instructions. Her farm supplied organic foods for the clients at her New York salons.

The rich America of the 1950s, released from tradition and class structures, seemed glamorous, especially to the young. They wanted to become that American phenomenon, the teenager. Brando depicted a defiant youth in *On the Waterfront*, James Dean a rebellious son in *East of Eden*. Musicals in Technicolor were exhilarating entertainment; sleek automobiles with flashing chrome were churned out by the motor industry; Coca-Cola and hot dogs constituted a comparatively exotic diet.

The Feminist Movement was established and growing in the United States. The novelist Truman Capote wrote sympathetically about a call girl in *Breakfast at Tiffany's* (though the film version would later blur her profession). The Abstract Expressionist painters, particularly Jackson Pollock, produced huge, radical images. Work from the Magnus photo agency was printed in lavishly illustrated magazines that explored unfashionable societies and landscapes, and these publications had a wide distribution, unsettling familiar notions about other cultures.

ABOVE: This purse seems to carry a conventional floral motif but a close inspection shows something else. The embroidered foliage is not familiar in shape, in fact, the design is drawn from Oriental artistic styles. It marks the beginning of a cultural mix caused by a growing global market.

Paris continued to dominate fashion, but it was threatened by these post-war developments. Fashion writers watched breathlessly to see if Dior would raise or lower hemlines, while Chanel's return to *haute couture* caused high excitement. Her suit, with its intricately cut jacket, was welcomed back by society women. In addition, *Vogue* announced that bags were getting bigger.

LEFT: The handbag business was not entirely geared to the young and radical, and Paris continued to influence concepts of chic, even among those who could not afford to buy from the great houses. This design (left) satisfied conventional ideas of style. Its shape is suited to the needs of most housewives; its fabric quiet in color and marked by demure stitching. It is satisfyingly large: its scale can be appreciated when seen carried by its owner (right).

RIGHT: This purse presents a delirious mix of natural and synthetic materials. The body is grass basket weave: on one surface, the weave frames an acrylic-covered picture that comprises seashells, embroidery, and textiles arranged to make a delightful underwater fantasy scene.

The elite, though, were not entirely cut off from ordinary people. Through *Vogue*, the fashion houses supplied sewing patterns of their complex designs so that women could attempt to make them at home. The lavish use of cosmetics was no longer regarded as vulgar, and articles covered subjects such as home hairdressing. Servants had disappeared from the labor pool, and even society women needed to do housework. Furthermore, travel by air and car ownership were no longer the privileges of the few. Conservative clothes and manners were under threat.

The majority of young women wanted to be lively and carefree, to be perceived as democratic and independent. The relaxed, sexy look was therefore "in," the elegant, dignified one most definitely "out."

RIGHT: This confection of wrought metal and great studded semi-precious stones represents a designer free to achieve his wildest handbag dream. Metal ducks' heads serve as clasps to hold a surprisingly unobtrusive transparent plastic handle. The creation was produced by the Dorset Rex company, and was meant, surely, for a frivolous, beautiful night out.

LEFT: The handle and clasp are acrylic with metal fixtures and the reverse side is adorned with a simple acrylic circle. It seems an accurate statement of the popular mood of the '50s.

145

1960s
EASY LIVING

Following the spirit of America, the young in Great Britain looked to artists to express their discontents. Dramatist John Osborne in his 1954 play *Look Back in Anger,* and the novelist John Braine in *Room at the Top*, were among the first to depict the anger of those who rejected the pre-war class system.

In 1960 the Italian filmmaker Fellini made the satire of modern Roman life, *La Dolce Vita*, and French filmmakers made clever, shocking movies such as *Jules et Jim*, which appeared in 1961. Sultry Italian beauties such as Gina Lollobrigida and Sophia Loren, who were neither aristocratic nor dignified in their looks, and the French actress, Jeanne Moreau, achieved a status similar to that of Hollywood stars. Elsewhere the Beatles were taking over popular music, once the domain of American artistes.

LEFT: European films emerged from the domination of Hollywood and they presented a different sense of glamour. The young French actress, Jeanne Moreau, had a world-weary air, quite different from the bright optimism of American stars.

RIGHT: Fashion began to show a penchant for color in defiance of the post-war subdued tones for daywear. Handbags made full use of the ever-improving technology of synthetic fabrics and dyes. This bold red purse with its gilt circles is a typical example. It comes from an anonymous American designer.

At the Paris Biennale of 1963, British artists such as David Hockney and Allen Jones were greeted with wild enthusiasm. They broke convention, shattering old stereotypes. Television proved a driving cultural force, showing irreverent programs mocking old fashioned conservative values. In the TV satire *That Was The Week That Was*, for example, many traditional institutions were savagely lampooned.

The U.S. and British economies were booming. Photography, film, and television opened up avenues of opportunity, welcoming creative people with or without classical university training. Fashion photographers such as David Bailey and Helmut Newton changed boundaries by showing models in sexy poses with tousled hair.

LEFT: This New York couple express the mood of exuberance that marked the '60s. His suit breaks all social conventions in male clothing, and her mini skirt and vanity case are a statement of a youthful attitude that ignored the standards set by the world fashion capital, Paris.

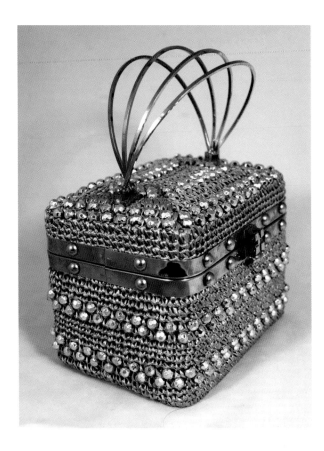

ABOVE: The four half-circle metal handles are also an innovative design touch. It was produced for the high end British market.

RIGHT: Heavy silver-colored raffia mesh decorated with glass baubles turn a sensible vanity case into a shiny evening accessory. The bag has the construction of a suitcase, including a lock clasp, but the materials and its neat size mock the bland appearance of the average travel case.

Paris lost control over the rhythm of women's clothing. The traditional pattern of seasonal collections was no longer relevant, and the new designers were not bothered by what was "correct." The English designer Mary Quant, who opened her boutique in 1955, leapt to the forefront of the 1960s fashion world. Hemlines were raised above the knee, and the coordinated ensemble was abandoned. In 1965 Quant presented a collection in New York City, and American fashionistas went wild with enthusiasm. Suddenly London was the center of new ideas and creative clothing.

151

Leiber

J udith Leiber (1921–) was the first woman to join the bagmakers guild in Budapest, Hungary. She fled the country during World War II, married an American GI, Gerson Leiber, and moved to New York. With her husband's support, she began to make handbags under her own name. Her work is meticulously handcrafted, aimed at the luxury market. Believing glamour should be displayed at all times, her handbags glitter with Swarovski crystals, rhinestones, and gold. Recalling the vanity cases and evening bags made by the jewelers of the 1930s, she creates hard-surfaced shapes covered in rich designs sparkling with color. Her most famous creation was the Minaudière, a little parcel in silver mesh tied with a gold mesh ribbon. Almost every U.S. president's wife since 1963 has carried a Leiber handbag to Inauguration ceremonies. Leiber retails exclusively through luxury store outlets.

ABOVE: Forced to leave her native Hungary under ugly circumstances, Judith Leiber chose to devote her work to the creation of glamorous and beautiful objects for women to enjoy. Her purses are proof of her creative optimism.

ABOVE: Leiber, essentially an artist, has the craftswoman's eye for detail. This can be seen in the use of a thin line of pink that gives a subtle finish to this handbag.

LEFT: The side panels of the bag add an unexpected flash of color on a seemingly demure evening clutch. The panels are of a different texture from the body and this, too, brings visual interest.

LEFT: A window display becomes a treasure chest of glittering shapes when filled with Judith Leiber's handbags. Gold, gleaming pearls, and crystals offer a dazzling choice for fashionistas searching for that very special handbag.

HANDBAGS

ABOVE: When the newly formed Coach leather works approached Bonnie Cashin to work with themy7, she told them her designs would be "as lightweight as possible—as simple as possible." One of her early handbags was this Classic shopper.

RIGHT: Cashin believed women used handbags to carry "stuff" and her products had exterior purses attached and were roomy enough for a magazine as well as a lipstick. She thought it was fine to carry two or three bags at a time if that's what was needed for "stuff." The model wittily exaggerates Bonnie's unconventional approach.

154

Handbags at this time were made in shiny PVC in hard bright colors. Initially, copycat Chanel 2.55 chain-handled clutches were preferred, but these were replaced by shopping bags with long chains to hook over a shoulder. Handbags were beaded plastic or silver with Perspex handles—materials suited to the informality of mini skirts and low heels.

BELOW: Once the bag is opened, the gilt trim forms a frame for interior fittings that hold cosmetics, and a mirror. The use of vanity bags as handbags was popularised when stars in Hollywood movies carried them in this way.

RIGHT: Plastic and vinyl are the materials used for this vanity case from Paris. The textured white plastic, set against the gleaming black vinyl, make for a sharp, smart, statement.

Bonnie Cashin's handbags epitomized the spirit of the 1960s. Women were working, participating in public life, and running their own households. Cashin gave them shoppers, totes, and the famous Cashin Carry. She scorned the conventional handbag, and gave her totes stitched-on pockets to store keys and change.

LEFT: Handbags were transformed during the '60s. Traditionally a minor fashion accessory, it became a useful object and made a statement. This plastic, basket weave style vanity case with ample space for accessories became very popular.

ABOVE: Women used handbags to serve many needs and with its divided interior and internal zipped purse, the owner could neatly pack her precious necessities. The handles and clasp are sturdy enough to withstand constant use.

LEFT: A model displays a Pucci catsuit that was shocking and amazing to many in her audience. New fabrics meant clothes could fit the human body better than before, but the model's casual use of a small tote bag was also unusual when carried with such a sumptuous outfit.

In Paris, André Courrèges made a collection that mixed the Space Age with designs based on the work of the abstract painter, Piet Mondrian. He used white and silver in trouser suits of lean pants and long, narrow coats. His skirts were above the knee and his blouses boxy. In London, meanwhile, Ossie Clark used black and white Op Art on quilted coats.

The Italian Emilio Pucci, famous for colorful shirts in the 1950s, brought the same gaiety to his handbags in the 1960s. He took Op Art and Art Deco and made swirling patterns in daring colors of avocado green, pink, and orange. His creations were sold in superior department stores.

RIGHT: Abstract paintings were the major art form of the late twentieth century, and it was matched by a general rejection of superfluous ornament. The big stripes and bright color of this vinyl purse drew on contemporary art for its inspiration.

Models were made up with pale lips and darkly accentuated eyes, while their hair was thick and high in the bouffant style. Their appearance reflected the camp culture of the New York artist, Andy Warhol. The wives of English rock stars, such as Bianca Jagger and Patti Boyd, were photographed endlessly, their images appearing in papers and magazines. Bianca was glamorous in couture, but Patti had a girlish appearance in trendy dungaree dresses. The model who took the fashion world by storm, however, was Twiggy. Waif-like and slender with an off-beat beauty, she perfected the "Dolly Girl" look of the decade.

LEFT: The English model, Twiggy, boards her flight to the USA where huge crowds greeted her. Her little girl appearance and casual style fitted with the growing power of the young. She carries a large bag with a wide firm base, perfect as a travel companion.

Pucci

The Italian Emilio Pucci (1914–1992) was an academic before turning to sportswear design, and went to the USA as a post-graduate student. A terrific skier, he designed for his college skiing team before returning to Capri. His work encapsulated the wild, synthetic advances of the 1960s and he loved to use technology in creating wrinkle-free fabrics. Color and bold design were his trademarks, and he was not inhibited by the comparatively small size of a handbag. He patterned them with large geometric motifs in unexpected color combinations. Although he catered for the high end of the market, his handbag designs were influential. They expressed modernity and new technology. Pucci designed the bag to carry a Sony Play Station portable gaming station. The Louis Vuitton-Moet-Hennessey Group bought the company in 1992.

BELOW: Pucci was not afraid to use large, swirling patterns on his bags and was recognized for his bold, unusual color schemes, as shown on this 1960s example.

RIGHT: Pucci is recognized as an innovative designer and the handbags shown in this shop window in Venice, Italy, are bold and colorful. Even in a fashion scene that is untrammeled and free, Pucci continues to make original and radical fashion statements.

LEFT: Emilio Pucci and a model, who wears black trousers designed as evening wear, a radical statement in the early 1960s.

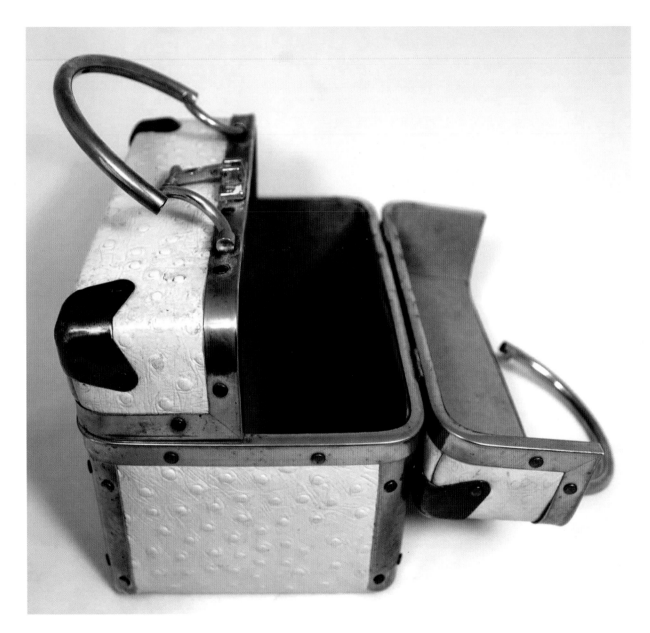

ABOVE: The numerous variations on the vanity case produced in the '60s proved the continuing popularity of this handbag shape. Here, the designer has created a dinky travel case in mock ostrich skin with robust brass corners and edges, and a lock clasp.

LEFT: The lid splits to give easy access to the deep interior, and this is lined with suede. This vanity case is chic and practical.

Naughty rich socialites and society girls bought Courrèges, Pucci, and the Quant style. Mary Quant was a radical dress designer, but her clothes were highly priced. She set off an avalanche of followers. Boutiques popped up all over London, and colors and cut changed with great rapidity.

In 1964 Barbara Hulanicki opened her influential boutique, Biba. She said, "I wanted to make clothes for people in the street." Hulanicki may have heard about the designer, McCardell. Certainly, her early work shadowed that of the American and revealed a similarly relaxed approach with minimal structure, relying on buttons, pockets, and color for style interest. And her clothes were inexpensive.

LEFT: Even the most conventional could not ignore the radical changes in fashion, and this high-end, crafted handbag in reptile skin pays quiet homage to contemporary notions of bold but minimal decoration.

BELOW: The buyer was reassured that her choice was not a wrong one when the bag's label, stitched into the interior lining, proved it came from one of the world's grandest department stores, Harrod's of London.

Biba's first garment was a drawstring evening skirt and her shop was bedecked with easy little dresses, A-line skirts, and jumpsuits. Her fabrics were tweedy looking or floral patterned, and her clothes were very cheap. They fitted the dolly image promoted by Quant. However, Hulanicki claimed that the demure expression, long neck, and slender figure of Audrey Hepburn inspired her, even though Twiggy was her favorite model.

Other America ideas drifted across the Atlantic. American hippies and Beatniks disassociated themselves from society, promoting an unconventional lifestyle outside the boundaries of work and family living. Jack Kerouac's book *On the Road* and Beat Poets such as Lawrence Ferlinghetti praised drug taking and sexual freedom. Furthermore, many Americans found themselves marginalized by their opposition to the United States' involvement in the Vietnam War. A strong underground culture developed and its influences were felt in Great Britain and Europe.

LEFT: Barbara Hulanicki was the driving force behind London's most popular boutique, Biba. She stands in her shop next to one of the Edwardian coat hangers on which she displayed her goods. Not only were her clothes radical, but her store was arranged in an unexpected manner with clothing, jewelery, and purses all mixed together and not placed within specific "department" areas.

British youth took to travel, and flirted with exotic cultures. The East became a magnet for the counterculture, and many took the hippy trail to Kathmandu, New Delhi, and Goa. These young travelers brought back an admiration for handicraft and a dislike of the industrialized world. They introduced a new element to fashion.

LEFT: The designer and illustrator, Enid Collins, paid little heed to fashion or trends. She hand painted her varnished papier mâché handbags and her images were eccentric and fanciful. This staring owl between sparkly stars is typical of her work. She signed each product as if it were an artwork, and discerning shoppers loved her purses. They are now highly valued by collectors.

night owl

RIGHT: Despite the variety shown in her handbag designs, Cashin never veered from practicality. The elegant simplicity of her purses combined with the company's quality craftsmanship ensured the lasting success of her handbags

Cashin

Bonnie Cashin, in her workshop, displays samples of her designs.

Bonnie Cashin designed costumes for a dance troupe in Los Angeles and worked for 20th Century Fox and various fashion houses before becoming an independent designer. Some of her first handbag designs were modeled on a paper bag. Many designs came in three sizes and she advocated layering one bag over another. Functionality was paramount and Cashin featured wide shoulder straps, large pockets, and industrial brass closures. Her handbags came in organic materials custom dyed to blend with her clothing designs each season.

Cashin worked closely with her leather workers, Philip Sills, and Coach owners Miles and Lillian Cahn, aiming to design for "modern nomads." Low-priced imitations were sold everywhere during the 1960s. After retiring from fashion in 1985, she set up the Innovative Design Award to fund prototypes related to clothing and domestic products. After her death in 2000, the Bonnie Cashin Foundation was established. A free spirit and keen traveler, Cashin refused to tie herself to one company and her label is now dormant. She established Bonnie Cashin Designs, Inc. in 1952 and closed her corporation in 1985—her influence continues to be enormous.

BELOW: Cashin preferred a soft structure which was comfortable to hold. She gave detailed thought to the bag's use and planned external pockets to allow easy access to keys and small change. Above all she avoided "fussiness." Decoration was generally confined to the metal of clasps and mounts.

COACH PRESENTS A NEW COLLECTION OF "CASHIN CARRY" BAGS AND ACCESSORIES DESIGNED BY BONNIE CASHIN

ABOVE: Her collaboration with the master leatherworks, Coach, inspired a witty advertisement. It shows that a girl can never own too many Cashin Carry bags.

Embroidered Afghan coats and tunics, carpet bags, beaded and mirrored skirts and blouses began to appear on the streets of London. The girls carried shoulder bags of cloth, heavily decorated with beads, sequins, and mirrors. Needlework of birds and flowers adorned their long skirts. Ex-army shoulder bags were touted about, hinting at dangerous but enlightening travel experiences.

RIGHT: The traditional floral motif is given glitzy treatment on this handbag. The sequins and glitter were taken from Oriental designs, but the free interpretation of the plants is modern Western. The handbag represents a fine blend of cultural identities. The motifs are appliquéd and embroidered on black felt. It was aimed at the high end of the American market.

Hulanicki captured the eclectic mood of the times. The interior of the Biba boutique was deliberately dim and mysterious, a seductive jumble of Art Nouveau, Art Deco, and the Arabian Nights. The staff had to control the crowds of young women who besieged the premises. The shoppers loved the short sac dresses, the feminine neo-1930s frocks patterned in Art Deco designs, and the long, dreamy dresses evoking Art Nouveau romance in a pre-mass production society.

LEFT: This Indian bag, crafted from various squares of embroidery, represented the mystery of India and her rich heritage of art. During the '60s, the country was a favorite destination for young western travelers who loved these easy tote bags bearing emblems of a romantic, exotic land. Handbags similar to this could be bought in markets and boutiques everywhere.

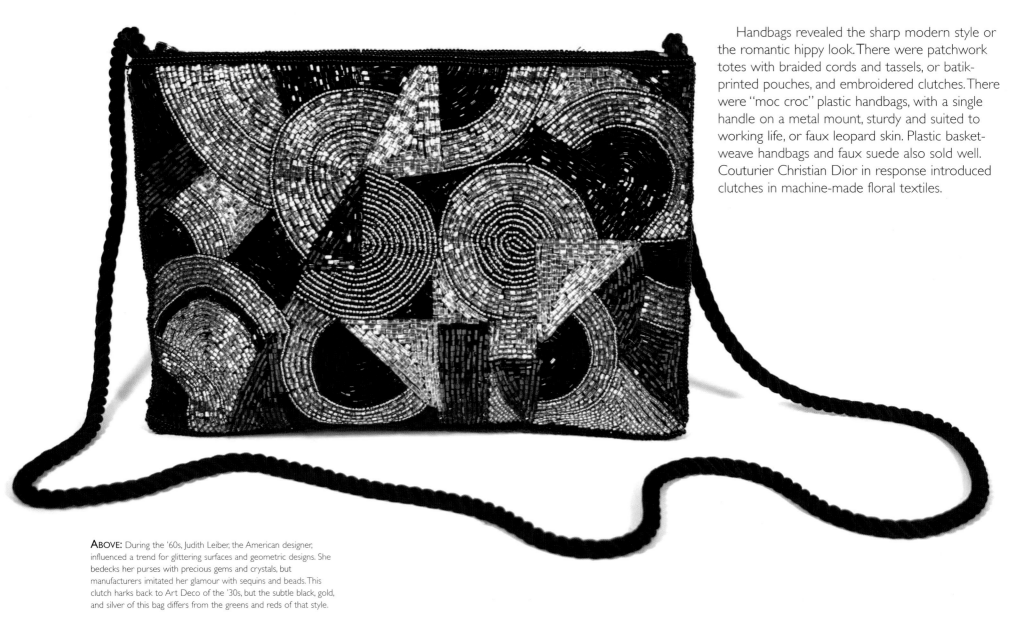

Handbags revealed the sharp modern style or the romantic hippy look. There were patchwork totes with braided cords and tassels, or batik-printed pouches, and embroidered clutches. There were "moc croc" plastic handbags, with a single handle on a metal mount, sturdy and suited to working life, or faux leopard skin. Plastic basket-weave handbags and faux suede also sold well. Couturier Christian Dior in response introduced clutches in machine-made floral textiles.

ABOVE: During the '60s, Judith Leiber, the American designer, influenced a trend for glittering surfaces and geometric designs. She bedecks her purses with precious gems and crystals, but manufacturers imitated her glamour with sequins and beads. This clutch harks back to Art Deco of the '30s, but the subtle black, gold, and silver of this bag differs from the greens and reds of that style.

The love of decoration, the glitter of sequins and embroidery found a partner in Judith Leiber. She used silk, crystals, and rhinestones, and her designs harked back to Art Deco. She saw no reason to confine glitter to evening wear and her 007 handbag, a sturdy box, had a bejeweled clasp and a glittering border hiding a secret compartment in the base.

The highly colorful fabrics of Zandra Rhodes and the drifting dresses of Celia Birtwell captured the mood for the high end of the market. Fashion and concepts of "what's in and what's out" had not entirely disappeared. In fact, the young had been determined to be cool and "with it," but the notion that fashion maintained a consensus of style dwindled as the decade came to a close. The fashion landscape became one of twists and turns, inhabited instead by a rich variety of styles.

LEFT: Soft velvets in rich colors; satin flowers, beads, and cords recall Pre-Raphaelite paintings, or Edwardian reticules. For young women who rejected bright, abstract modernity, preferring instead dreamy, nostalgic clothing, this drawstring pouch was a perfect choice. Brenda Duval, a South African designer made the bag. This decade saw the start of a varied, global market in fashion.

1970s
ANYTHING GOES

I n 1970 the American ecologist Rachel Carson wrote *Silent Spring*, a lyrical, terrifying account of the dangers of industrial pollution. *The Whole Earth Catalogue* by Stewart Brand, published in 1972, was a thick handbook filled with information for those who wanted to live in an ecologically sound manner. It listed tools and methods of building and crop growing to help individuals function outside the corporate system. Both books found groups of disciples, and during the 1970s the USA saw the growth of communes whose members rejected the modern world for one of home-grown food, handmade clothes, and simple living.

RIGHT: The young rebelled against the power of couture Paris and radical English designers were suddenly in control. In London, independent boutiques made and sold youthful fashions showing short hemlines, bold color, and designs drawn from cultures across the world. Bus Stop was one of the more daring and successful of these fashion outlets.

HANDBAGS

RIGHT: With its fringing and color images, this bag pays homage to Native American methods and styles in leatherwork. Western designers of the '70s were interested in using artistic motifs outside their own tradition.

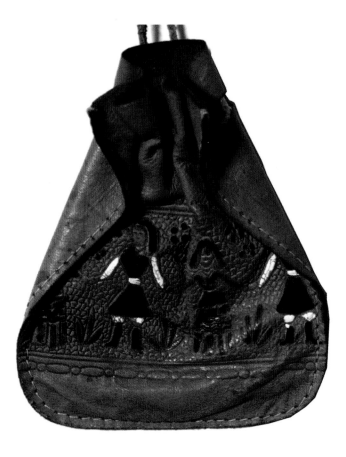

ABOVE: A matching purse of the same style was a handy accessory for the beautifully decorated bag.

These anti-establishment views were exploited by the fashion world. The ecological/hippy look was seen everywhere, and designers revealed an appreciation of the craftwork championed by this minority. The English designer Jean Muir made handbags with leather appliqué. In high street shops and boutiques, machine-embroidered or patchwork bags proved to have a big market. "Squaw" bags—large, loose pouches that were beaded, fringed, and tasseled—looked handmade, implying a rejection of machine production. Even structured leather handbags appeared in patchworks of many colors.

LEFT: The leather workshop of Ackery translated the patchwork "hippy" look in the design of their snakeskin handbags and purses. It made a fashionable statement but the careful patchwork was neither radical nor haphazard.

LEFT: This youthful shopper epitomizes the carefree mood of popular fashion. Her dress is unstructured and her hair has not been styled. And she swings a handbag from a long strap designed to hook on her shoulder.

BELOW: This woven leather handbag, adorned with a bold buckle, is designed to hang from the shoulder. Its capacious size and strong color combination is typical of the everyday bags popular during this decade.

The 1970s also saw the beginning of computer technology and increased productivity from manufacturers. In Great Britain trade unions fought to maintain jobs made redundant by the new technology, while the working classes began to enjoy the advantages—central heating, air travel, processed food, and cheap clothing. *Vogue* remarked that life had become so busy that women dressed in five minutes and their wardrobe was reduced to an easy mix of separates.

Synthetics could look like tweed or satin and were washable and wrinkle free. Oxford bags and cardigans were part of the new informality, as were leather or mock-leather shoulder bags which had saddle stitching and long wide shoulder straps. Canvas, too, was favored, carrying leather trim and dog-leash fittings. The bags were firmly structured and smart.

RIGHT: There was a trend for colorful or patchwork handbags, but the market for carefully constructed, well made bags never goes away. This pale leather has been designed with a deep mount, allowing the bag to be opened wider than usual. It was not intended for the youth market.

BELOW: Designed for the 2010 season, metal rivets are threaded with cords, apparently holding in one piece, this big, loose pouch.

RIGHT: On this snakeskin 2010 season handbag Falchi has made a ribbon of the skin to thread through the drawstring neck. The casual, soft shapes are also typical of his work..

Falchi

As a youthful, hippy designer in New York, Carlos Falchi made leather trousers and bags by hand and dyed the leather in his bathtub. Initially he rejected the structured craft of traditional European bag makers, and in 1970 he produced his Buffalo bag, which was cut from a single skin and had one seam. Its large size, in leather soft enough to "squash and trash," appealed to all levels of the market. Tina Turner and Elvis Presley bought his work, while factories made thousands of cheap copies.

Falchi's recent work has assumed a structured approach although his shapes—hexagons and narrow oblongs, for instance—are unusual. He uses colored leather, feathers, and combinations of raw edges and macramé decoration while pursuing innovative tanning techniques and inventive finishes. An ecologist, he uses material from sustainable sources. He is still based in New York.

LEFT: Carlos Falchi has always been bold in his use of acidrock color, and his original methods of seaming and tying his handbags are instantly recognizable.

BELOW: In response to the market, or perhaps to satisfy his own creative needs, Falchi turned to structured shapes. His fascination with surface textures and the nature of leather itself diverted him, and even in the more conventional design of this handbag, he could not resist letting the material fall into soft folds and corners.

For the first time in the West, merchants and producers were not wooing the rich. As the commentator Alistair Cook remarked, "Fashionable people were all right but they were not a mass market." For now the profits were to be made by selling to the broad mass of working people. Those voices that warned of the dangers of pollution, sprawling cities, and environmental destruction were largely ignored. Shoppers enjoyed the fruits of the industrial output. They were happy to have the comforts promised by the factories. Nevertheless, the mood was not as carefree or reckless as that of the 1960s.

RIGHT: Jays of Bond Street made this black leather handbag, conventional in design but the unobtrusive stitched decoration gives it an individual flourish. The mount has been covered by leather and the gilt clasp adds a small dash of discreet color.

LEFT: Bright color suits this jaunty barrel-shaped bag. It has a shoulder strap but this can be removed so that the bag may be carried on a short single handle. The clasp is a snatch latch, and its decorative quality fits the star studs along the opening edge. This was a bag for a young mass market.

Bonnie Cashin was in the habit of drawing and writing notes directly on to the bag prototypes she prepared for the manufacturer but here is a note to potential customers. She let's them know that they are purchasing a useful weatherproof bag. This canvas bag was commissioned by the company, D.Klein.

BELOW: The Mail Box, designed in 1974, did all the things a handbag should do—according to Bonnie Cashin. It was "a container to carry all the stuff a girl seems to need." The handy exterior purses were much appreciated by the many women who bought the Mail Box.

The oil crisis of 1973, when prices shot up, affected trade and manufacture. Unemployment figures rose. The housewife was becoming an endangered species: more and more women in the USA and Britain sought paid employment. And "working wives" continued to be a matter of debate because conservatives saw this development as a danger to family life. Of course, women lived as the times demanded, and most welcomed the changes. Many remembered rationing and had grown up in poor housing. They were glad they and their daughters had more control over their destinies. And they enjoyed the increased availability of manufactured clothes and plastic handbags.

In the 1970s, Bonnie Cashin continued designing for Coach and adapting functional designs from seemingly unrelated source material. Her whimsical "Mailbox" shoulder bag featured exterior pockets that opened like a mailbox at each end, while her "Mail Sacks" were kin to traditional mail carriers work bags. Beginning in 1975, Cashin began designing her trademark leather bags with toggle clasps for Meyers, and in the late 1970s she also designed lines of canvas totes for D. Klein, many bearing prints of her own design with a hand-written statement from Cashin reprinted on the interior. Her work managed to capture an informal but chic modernity. They served the on-the-go woman, whether for business or leisure.

LEFT: Bags as portable slings, easy to carry and soft enough to mold against the body's contours—Cashin's first totes fulfilled these demands. The designer did not abandon her beliefs in handbags as easy to carry and useful for storage. These totes were made for D. Klein. Their shapes and offbeat color mix are typical of Bonnie Cashin's work.

The movies revealed a relaxed moral attitude, expressing the changes in the role of women and traditional values. *A Touch of Class* with Glenda Jackson was a kindly, comic view of adultery, and the thriller *Klute*, with Jane Fonda, was a sympathetic depiction of a prostitute's life. Meanwhile, Germaine Greer sold 75,000 copies of her book, *The Female Eunuch*, a bible for the women's movement. In photographs of the time, Greer's hair is thick, long, and carefree, and her clothes have a gipsy glamour that signal she is an ecologist.

LEFT: The actress, Jane Fonda, presents an image far removed from the old-time Hollywood glamour icon. Her clothes are easy in line and her handbag resembles a small hold-all, spacious and relaxed.

LEFT: This soft bag has no mount but a wrap-over cover conceals an inner pocket, big enough to fit a paperback. A zip closure guards a roomy interior and the lack of a metal mount means the bag hangs comfortably against the hip.

Delvaux

Charles Delvaux opened a leather studio in Belgium in 1829. Within a few years, the Belgian royal family appointed him supplier of their luggage and bags. In 1933 Franz Schwennicke purchased the firm. The high standard of workmanship was not altered but changing styles were largely ignored. Schwennicke's wife, Solange, changed this during the 1970s by modernising the company. Today her son François and his CTO Christian Salez run the company and, though output from Delvaux remains small, its designs are sleek and contemporary. The current artistic director is Veronique Branquinho and she works with designers such as Bruno Pieters and Hannelore Knuts. Despite its exclusive market, Delvaux is sold in outlets across the world. Every bag is cut and stitched by highly trained craftsmen and the company's status has been recognised in a recent exhibition in the Mode Museum, Antwerp.

RIGHT: The Delvaux house has worked hard to lift its image from a small Belgium company to a modern brand in the global market. This advertisement confirms that they have achieved this recognition.

DELVAUX
BRUXELLES
Established since 1829. The Leather trail.

BRUSSELS · ANTWERP · PARIS · MONTE CARLO · LUXEMBURG · TOKYO · SINGAPORE · NEW YORK

DELVAUX-CREATEUR

● collection plein-soleil

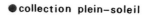

ABOVE: The Delvaux house now produces contemporary bags for the global market; here emphasising its youth appeal.

RIGHT: Delvaux maintains steady sales of designs dating from the 1950s, and clients rely on the superb craftsmanship of each product. The cutting and assembling techniques have not altered for generations. In the image on the right, a craftsman pares the edge of a leather bag, ensuring a smooth, malleable quality. The fine leather interior pocket lining can also be seen.

But a reluctance to accept change could also be seen in dreamy, floral clothes that expressed a longing for a gentle femininity rather than Feminism. *Vogue* carried photographs of rural fantasies and picnics, showing women in long skirts and blouses with full sleeves. The models carried basket bags or embroidered linen shoulder bags. They posed as gardeners wearing tweed and cardigans fashioned as *faux* country wear.

RIGHT: Germaine Greer was the voice of feminism and demanded a change in the way women were viewed. She dared to say handbags were unnecessary but, although her influence was considerable, few women were prepared to abandon this precious accessory, one that served a useful, intimate purpose in their lives.

Factory output concentrated on pastel-colored leather or plastic handbags, while Clive Shilton designed floral-printed clutches for the major stores. *Haute couture* houses turned to exquisite Chinese embroidery on satin drawstring bags, and the lower end of the market imitated these. All these designs hinted at nostalgia, a longing for simpler times and a slower domestic life. Bonnie Cashin's Coach bag, an elegant shopper, came in a range of bright clear colors and somehow combined the hippy look with metropolitan smartness and sass.

LEFT: A romantic backward look to gentle images of women provoked some designers to produce soft fabric purses with handles attached by stitching, thus avoiding any hard clasps or mounts. Here, a pink plastic "jewel" is fitted onto the zipper closure.

LEFT: The Delvaux leatherworks in Brussels employs forty-five craftsmen. Here, they cut and assemble by hand the structured handbags for which the company is famous. The Pub shoulder bag is typical of their careful seaming and design detail.

BELOW: The Corfou purse has a less formal appearance and is aimed at a younger clientele. Both were made in 1973. The company's trademark is a reminder of its beginnings in the far-off days of leather saddlery for coach and horses.

Despite the advances in technology, the old of craft of leatherwork continued in the workshops of Ferragamo, Fendi, and the House of Delvaux in Belgium. Their bags were monogrammed, and cream and dark brown were the preferred colors. Initially, shoulder bags and firm purses predominated but big, soft clutches grew popular. Handmade leather bags were available in street markets but they were usually of a basic envelope shape and clumsy in their handicraft. Many were embossed and colored by the hippy craftsmen who made them.

Clothes were chosen to reflect the wearer's life. The ecologist who cared for the natural world wore long skirts or ethnic outfits, and her purse was a fabric shoulder bag. The professional woman, on the other hand, wore layers of tweed and wool and carried a capacious, pouchy handbag slung over her shoulder.

LEFT: The finely grained markings of lizard skin add to the quiet luxury of this bag made by Debroyal. The woman who bought this handbag wanted to convey that her life was dignified, calm, and secure. She did not need to attract attention or make bold statements through her accessories.

191

Mulberry

BELOW: This large pouchy handbag in warm tones is a hallmark Mulberry design. The leather is of the highest quality, cleverly cut and sewn to expresses practicality and handsome good looks.

LEFT: The clasp is designed to be locked, and a neat little leather tube is tied to the handle so that the padlock and keys have a handy storage place.

With the help of his mother, Roger Saul opened a leather workshop called Mulberry in the English town of Bath in 1971. Initially he exported his belts to Australia, but soon he was selling belts and chokers through Biba and Jean Muir, and in 1974 he opened his own outlet in London. By 1975 he was designing and making handbags for the couture house Kenzo and the luxury department store Bloomingdale's in New York. His handbags fitted the market for English country elegance. Superbly crafted, they were "romantic but robust" in mood, and sturdy in structure. Hunting bags and the like were his inspiration, and his purses were prized for their "witty English eccentricity." Recognized for quality leather products and excellent design, Mulberry now has outlets in twenty-one different countries and is sold through luxury outlets in Britain such as Selfridges and Liberty.

LEFT: The truncated trees displaying Mulberry bags is a witty reference to their English country style. But the window shows the true variety of the company's products from roomy hold-alls to neat handbags.

RIGHT: Printing technology was considerably improved during the '70s, and color images were much easier to produce on fabrics as well as paper. Handbag designers, always willing to experiment with new materials and techniques, combined color and printing to create a magazine bag.

ABOVE: Everyone folds a magazine to carry it about. Cleverly, the designer folded his magazine bag, holding it closed with a leather strap. The end result makes for colorful narrow clutches.

The luxury consumer chose saddlebags or stuck to trusted classics from Vuitton and Chanel. Workshops at this end of the market, such as the House of Delvaux, knew the rich had not abandoned their longing for elegance. Modern designers came from new workshops under designers such as Carlos Falchi and Roger Saul of Mulberry. Their products were contemporary and maintained a superior standard of production.

People went straight from the office to the cinema, theater or concert hall, so few working women had time to change or bother with an evening bag. Those who did preferred one less showy than of old; for this market Christian Dior made unadorned suede or satin clutches with long chains hooked over the shoulder.

LEFT: Garfields, the makers of this handbag, have made an interesting seam along the base and the neat straps emphasize the width of the bag. There is always a market for this level of craftsmanship.

Fashion reflected the schisms in the cultural consensus. Feminism had a powerful voice and increasingly women freed themselves from deeply held notions of modesty. Some chose to exhibit these views by rejecting cosmetics and the right clothes for the right occasion. Jeans, T-shirts and army style bags were worn in the high street and the concert hall. Even movie stars dropped their glamorous image occasionally: Jane Fonda, gorgeous sex symbol of the science fiction film *Barbarella*, faced the world's press in unsexy, tired travel trousers to talk about the Vietnam War.

BELOW: This is an example of the work of a practical designer. The pouch has a deep handle that has been fitted into side panels of a leather-like fabric. This tough synthetic material is able to withstand the constant opening and closing of the bag, unlike the prettier but more delicate weave that covers the rest of the bag.

LEFT: These young women huddle under blankets at a wet pop festival in the '70s. They are dashingly fashionable in the "hippy" vogue, but in place of a purse, one girl uses a plastic bag supplied to shoppers by the famous Biba boutique. Its distinctive logo adds a certain cachet to the style of this youthful fashionista.

Handbag designers were no different from men and women working in other sectors of the fashion industry. By the time the Vietnam War ended in 1973, they were compelled to find a market place in a changing society where tastes were, to say the least, unpredictable.

BELOW: This delightful clutch in warm colors has the appearance of a handwoven textile, and the acrylic mount imitates the rich markings of wood. The "natural" look fulfilled the preferences of shoppers, and mass production techniques made it available for many young customers.

HANDBAGS

RIGHT: The then Prime Minister of Britain, Mrs Thatcher, is seen here with President Reagan and his all-male entourage at a 1980s press conference. Her opponents mocked her by claiming she used her handbag, that essentially female accessory, as a weapon to frighten her male colleagues. However, many women admired her style, and large handbags became a fashion item.

1980s
BOLD AND BRASSY

At the dawn of the 1980s, ecologists and hippies were thrust aside as affluence spread across the industrialized world. Many people were now enjoying access to money, goods, and property undreamt of by previous generations—and they liked it. The Feminists had broken down many barriers, and women were now part of the world of work. In Britain a female Prime Minister, Margaret Thatcher, showed a belief in capitalism that matched the popular mood, and the people voted for her in three successive elections.

The sense of female power was strengthened by two American TV soap dramas. *Dallas* and *Dynasty* depicted assertive, rich women who were not cowed by men. The stars dressed extravagantly in suits of hard, flat color with big shoulder pads and short skirts worn with high heels. They carried Chanel's quilted bag or Vuitton's luggage handbags, and female viewers wanted the same. The chic but "boho" ethnic look was abandoned.

Barbara Taylor Bradford wrote bestselling novels about women who, through their own efforts, achieved riches and prestige. Her women were an unexpected side effect of Feminism. The sisterhood's fight for gender equality did not drive these heroines: they preferred self-determination.

Karl Lagerfeld, chief designer for Chanel, caught the mood. The quilted clutch grew to the size of a briefcase. It was made of shiny patent leather, dangled on heavy chains, and bore the Chanel "CC" logo in huge gilt letters. Loud and assertive, it expressed the persona of female executives. Alternatively, they could carry a woven leather clutch with ostentatious gilt chains from Bottega Veneta or Gucci's showy Pasta bag.

RIGHT: Handbags assumed a strong no-nonsense shape, suited to a serious career. This patent crocodile skin with metal rivets proved a popular seller on the high street.

LEFT: Successful women wore crisp, co-ordinated outfits, implying efficiency and logic. This ensemble comes from the 1983 collection of Jean-Louis Scherrer. Color-matched to the outfit, the large clutch purse was an essential element in creating the carefully planned over-all effect.

BELOW: The mesh surface of this handbag has a glamorous shimmer, and the gold metal handle adds to the effect. However, it is shaped like a standard male briefcase, indicating that the woman carrying it is both gorgeous and serious.

Ambitious office girls copied the look. The coordinated elegance of the 1950s returned, although the mood was not so ladylike. Hair was no longer tousled, but arranged to form a high, thick frame around the face and neck. Bold gold earrings and necklaces were worn with suits and cocktail dresses: the formality of occasion dressing had returned.

LEFT: Handbag manufacturers offered a wide choice and women did not have to look business-like all the time. Goldpfeil made this textile purse in apple green with a thick single handle so that the wearer could swing her purse, casual and easy, from her wrist.

BELOW: The world of popular music was as influential as that of business, and pop was carefree and vibrant. This faux suede handbag implied the light, artistic personality of the wearer, different from that of an ambitious career girl.

LEFT: Chanel's celebrated 2/1955 quilted bag was jazzed up by designer, Karl Lagerfeld, in the 1980s, and of course, the manufacturers appropriated his variations. This quilted disco Chanel style bag is adorned with a showy chain handle of twined gold and silver metal links.

Moschino

Franco Moschino (1950-1994) worked for Armani before starting his company—initially named Moonshadow—in 1983. By nature Franco was rebellious, witty, and clever, and his designs were irreverent and imaginative. One handbag, structured and conservative in shape, was cream with the appearance of chocolate dripping down its sides. And the Moschino backpack was molded as a woman's corset, black lace on red, the curvaceous bust serving as the opening to the interior. His handbags were finely crafted and delighted young women who felt they expressed their own sense of irony. He never ceased to take pleasure in spoofing consumerism and the big corporations, so was embarrassed to find himself listed among the top most successful designers. Moschino was a strong ecologist and a portion of his company profits are donated to charities around the world.

RIGHT: In this window display gorgeous clothes and luxurious handbags are packed onto a humble three-wheeled delivery vehicle, a familiar form of transport across the Mediterranean.

BELOW: This soft surfaced purse has been quilted with hearts and peace signs, familiar symbols in an unfamiliar setting: the kind of contrast that delights Moschino. Adding a further unsettling note, the big links of the chain handles hint at brutality.

LEFT: Moschino takes a witty swipe at the old fashion rule that accessories must match your outfit. His hat, dress, and bag are all of the same patterned fabric, and the bag is festooned with chains and handcuff bracelets, implying the strict confinement of fashion diktats.

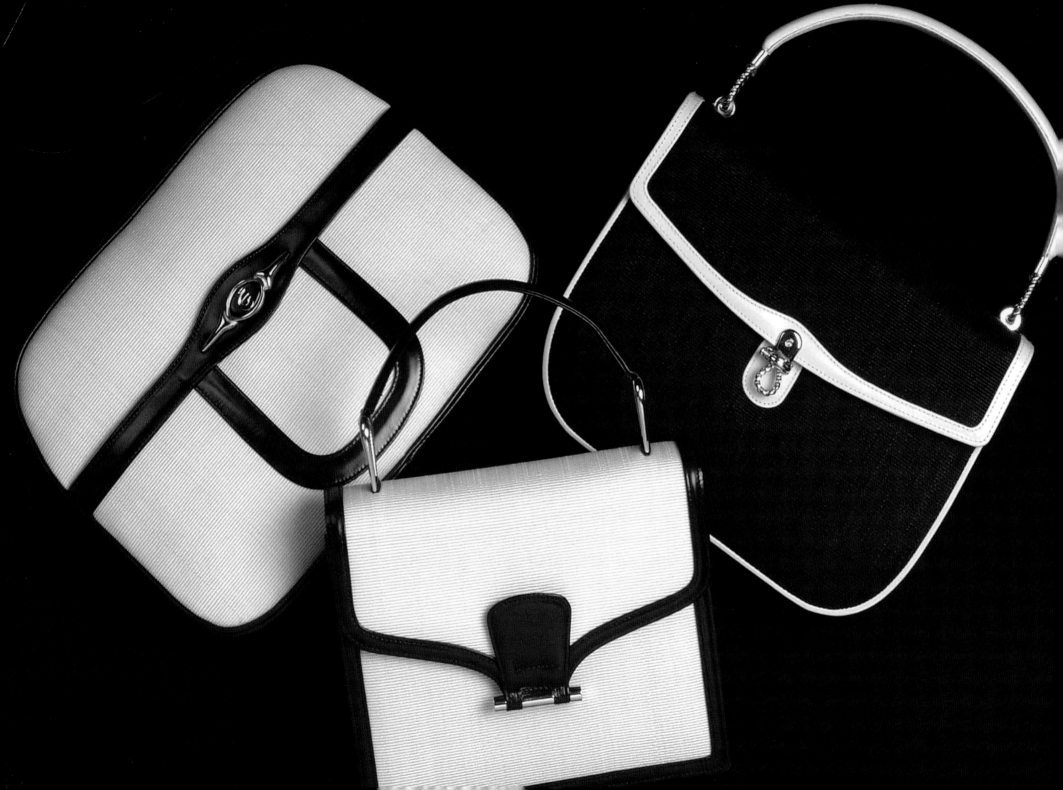

LEFT: The designs of these handbags are graphic, neat and pleasing. They represent a delight in symmetry and a calm good sense, matching the attitudes of most women. The bags were made in Germany.

The handbags matched the shoes. Dull gold, silver, and pewter were preferred as tones to fit strongly colored ensembles. The bags were carried in the hand or tucked under the arm. A large clutch could be carried with a big-shouldered suit or evening jacket of brocade, gold lamé, or lace. The bags were enriched with appliquéd decoration, or else the leather was braided or worked with basket weave.

Of course, the social stratum of "old money" did not vanish but it had begun to shrink alarmingly. These people patronized craftsmen such as Vuitton, who designed the Birkin bag, a deep practical handbag with a demure gilt buckle. They bought the classic Hermès Kelly bag, now in strong colors, and looked for products from couture houses such Chanel and Christian Dior.

But there was another style, very different from that of Mrs Thatcher or the stars of *Dynasty*. Lady Diana Spencer was beautiful and photogenic, and as the young bride of the Prince of Wales she cut a romantic figure. Her wedding dress and subsequent ball gowns were Cinderella dreams of huge skirts and puffed sleeves. The Princess of Wales wore soft, silky fabrics often patterned with clear color combinations. Her shoes were low and her demeanor modest.

LEFT: Diana, Princess of Wales, preferred a soft romantic style to the sharp business suit. Her fashion influence was to be enormous, and because she carried clutches they became a major fashion trend. Here, she tucks a big fold-over clutch under her arm.

BELOW: Manufacturers responded quickly to the demand for soft, pouchy clutches. These purses were mass-produced in a wide range of colors and they came in synthetic fabric with plastic mounts and clasps.

Her extravagant evening wear, though, was echoed by the wildly romantic gear adopted by rock musicians. David Bowie and Adam Ant appeared in dandified Regency coats or pranced about in dress-up pirate costumes. Boy George wore cosmetics and elaborately decorated jackets. These rock stars found their fashion muse in the unorthodox Vivienne Westwood, whose designs were eye-catching but wildly impractical.

The fashion world gaped at the exuberance of color, texture, and daring in the work of Gianni Versace, and the witty irreverence of Jean-Charles de Castelbajac. Such artistry reflected the breaking of barriers in tradition and "good taste."

In the USA the young singer Madonna appeared with a mass of hair tied up in ribbons, her clothes a mix of lace and leather. Hers was a statement of carefree individuality. Even Norman Parkinson, whose long career serves as a style barometer, made images of women in scarlet gowns as frilled and flounced as the costume of a flamenco dancer. Or else the models rested their huge waves of hair against the frothy collar of an evening gown.

RIGHT: There was a backlash against grand statements of power and money. Handbags carrying whimsical motifs were favored by some designers and here, the charms that usually dangle from a chain bracelet are used to decorate a bag surface.

The makers of crafted leather sensed profit lay in extending their market beyond old-style elegance. The family businesses and *haute couture* houses started selling their "brands." The logo of the brand would reveal the shopper's wealth, discernment, and fashion savvy. Handbags became a competitive sign among women who wanted to announce their financial status. When a new purse from Gucci or Vuitton was announced, long queues formed at luxury outlets for the latest "It" bag.

The American writer Tom Wolfe satirized this culture of greed and consumer snobbery in his novel *The Bonfire of the Vanities* which was set in Manhattan, the heart of consumerism. Although it was a major bestseller, the book caused hardly a dent in the shopping frenzy. Fashion reached into every area of life, even sportswear was affected.

LEFT: The Gladstone bag is the classic of all bags, being one of the earliest designs prompted by the needs of lady travelers on the first railroads. It was named in honour of the Victorian statesman, Gladstone. It enjoyed a revival, such as this version, in the 1980s when large, sturdy handbags were demanded by businesswomen, many of whom were obliged by their work to travel frequently by air.

RIGHT: Excess was praised and "greed is good" was the mantra. Champagne and luxury accessories, such as the leather bucket bag that can be glimpsed behind the fine leather loafers and perfume bottles, were envied and admired.

Prada

The Italian company Prada started life as a quality leather workshop. Like many other family firms, it struggled to cope with the global economy of the late twentieth century. In 1978 Miuccia Prada, grandchild of the founder, controlled the design department. With her husband Patrizio Bertelli she modernized the company. For many years, Prada had been making a waterproof backpack, but in 1985 Miuccia revamped this practical hiker's product into a version that was both handbag and backpack.

The company moved into couture in 1989 and a subsidiary group, Miu Miu, was formed for the lower end of the market. Prada is a leader in research into synthetic fabrics—for instance, its innovative beaded latex. The Council of Fashion Designers of America awarded Miuccia Prada its prize for best design in 1993. The company continues to produce much sought-after luxury handbags.

LEFT: The vibrant colors and "boho chic" that identify the house of Prada is on full show in this window display. The bold handbags are very much part of this style.

RIGHT: Miuccia Prada made the brave decision to re-vamp the family's respected traditional output. Her own style, modern, chic, and relaxed was translated into practical, fashionable handbags for a modern market. Working with her husband, Patrizio Bertelli, she has given Prada a major role in the fashion world.

LEFT: Prada is renowned for experimentation and research into leather and synthetic fabrics. This handbag shows the advances made by the company in both color effects and textures. The unexpected brown handles, fitted against pink and orange, add the twist that Prada brings to their designs.

LEFT: The bumbag proved hugely popular, although it lacked elegance and certainly was not chic. But the design—a purse tied firmly round the wearer's waist—catered to fears of robbery while abroad, or loss during the kerfuffle of travel and because it is handy to have money and keys securely tied up leaving both hands free.

Sports clothes inspired research, and textiles of extraordinary strength and flexibility became available. Light in weight and easy to maintain, Spandex and Lurex stretched and hugged the body. Women took to wearing leggings with a long loose shirt or long jacket. Tracksuits intended as warm-up garments for sportsmen were translated into shell suits for suburban mothers.

Travel was no longer confined to the rich or to hippies. Many people could afford to catch a cheap flight to Florida, Greece, Turkey, or even Vietnam. Shell suits in pastel shades were preferred for travel wear. Bum bags, small pouches stitched to a belt, were tied around the waist so the wearers could be confident their money was secure in dangerous foreign lands. Vuitton produced robust canvas luggage-style bags to be carried on board planes.

LEFT: The interior of this travel bag is arranged to hold pens, passports, credit cards, and the like. It's robust appearance in hardwearing tan leather makes it perfectly suited to its purpose.

Credit was available even on modest incomes, and banks authorized credit cards to thousands of consumers. Debts swelled as properties were bought on mortgage and goods purchased on "plastic." Those symbols of wealth, the Chanel and the Birkin bags, were easily acquired. In response couture houses offered ever-larger bags with long straps, pockets, and buckles.

As the decade progressed, the extravagant look overwhelmed the fashion pages. Pop musicians, footballers, tennis players, and golfers flaunted their great wealth. Young working women purchased, no doubt on credit, the Chanel 2.55 bag now appearing in denim, rubber, and terry cloth. Moschino presented witty handbags, decorated with gilt, mocking the fashion for big bags. The young rich snapped them up.

RIGHT: The sleek quality leather and clever cut of this shopper proclaimed the expensive shopping habits of the wearer. The gilt button, with a gem inset, adds extra emphasis.

Throughout the decade, the lives and clothes shown in TV shows like *Dallas* remained hugely influential. Handbags were used to convey elegance with a whiff of wealth, as with this subtle suede saddlebag carried by heavy chain links.

Bottega
Veneta

Michele Taddei and Renzo Zengiaro formed this company in Vicenza, Italy, in 1966. They concentrated on structuring leather, weaving, and braiding the material, though their purse designs were unstructured and relied on the woven surface to give decoration. Each bag was hand-woven and light-nuanced neutral tones were preferred. Their work sold steadily throughout the 1980s when consumers were ready to pay very high prices, but faltered in the late 1990s. Giles Deacon was brought in to re-vamp the company and update the products. He successfully introduced a ready-to-wear couture brand. In 2001 the designer Tom Ford persuaded his employers, Gucci, to buy the company. Bottega Veneta was entrusted to another design director, Tomas Maier and it was through his work that the company reclaimed its position in the luxury leather market.

RIGHT: This design house moves with dexterity from the conventional to the experimental. The rich color and sober shape of this handbag represents their more conventional aspect, but the richness of the color, offset by touches of gilt, lifts it above the average.

LEFT: The model carries the kind of bag associated with Bottega Veneta, that is, pouchy, relaxed, and made in soft colors. It is worth noting the bag has a broad handle, making it very comfortable to carry.

BELOW: Bottega Veneto have long been admired for their woven leather work. This way of using leather creates interesting surfaces that are effective on a large bag, as in the red drawstring tote, or on the small surface of the black clutch.

Female rock stars bought work from new designers such as Prada and Bottega Veneta, or they turned to Westwood or Jean-Charles de Castelbajac for outrageous outfits that would wow the crowd. Girls going to discos wanted to look bold and eccentric just like Madonna. Thierry Mugler responded to their demand by making small bags in ball or hexagonal shapes of firm, shiny fabrics that could withstand the wild dancing.

BELOW: A pink canvas shopper is given the full glamour treatment expected in the handbags of the 1980s. Sequinned straps and decoration make it more than a simple everyday shopping bag, and it could be used happily as an on-board air travel bag as well.

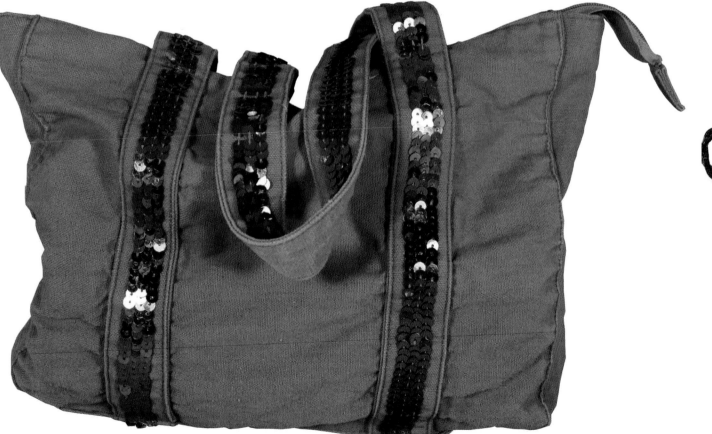

ABOVE: The successful designer, Thierry Mugler, designed a multi-faceted patent ball for disco dancing. This coconut bag, zipped round its middle, comes from Brazil, and its hard surface and zany appearance made it a perfect accessory at the disco.

RIGHT: This shining silver mesh clutch was designed to go disco dancing. The long chain handle allowed the handbag to hang across the chest or from the shoulder while the wearer cavorted on the dance floor.

Sportsmen had become celebrities and people yearned for healthy, well-toned bodies. They walked to work, went jogging, and flocked to gyms. Women wanted bags to hold accessories of an active life such as sports shoes, bulky Filofax diary, pens, purse, and cosmetics. Shoulder bags didn't meet the demand. Then in 1985 Prada made a black nylon backpack. Elegant and simple, it had pockets, internal compartments, and a roomy interior. It was instantly copied. Smart women toted smart backpacks in place of purses or shoppers.

As the decade advanced, big fashion corporations dominated the market, promoting their products with relentless publicity campaigns. Status was judged less by position in society than by the flaunting of a fashion logo.

RIGHT: A sumptuous gold and black clutch with a narrow gold mount and handle was a grand statement of the wealth and excess of the decade. But it is beautifully styled, conveying, also, taste and elegance.

LEFT: Prado designed an elegant riposte to the bumbag when they made a neat triangular handbag with two straps to hook over the shoulders. There were many copies, like this version. With a sturdy clasp and hanging close against the wearer's back, the wearer felt their possessions were secure while their hands were free. It was wildly successful and soon moved into larger versions worn by both men and women.

1990s
BIG BRAND MANIA

During the 1990s, manufacture moved away from its established base in Western Europe and the USA. Computer technology allowed factories to design, cut, and assemble goods considerably faster than had been possible before. Any department store could commission its own products from factories in China, Vietnam, and India, where labor was cheap. The retailers would spot style trends from the *haute couture* houses, copy them, have them made quickly in the Far East, and in the stores within days.

LEFT: The singer and actress, Madonna was known as "The Material Girl." Her brash style, and her refusal to recognize any of the conventional barriers made her the icon of the decade. Her outrageous clothes and confidence encouraged many young women towards self-expression in their lives and fashion.

HANDBAGS

The bold style of the 1980s was abandoned. Career women continued to wear suits, but these were freed of huge shoulder pads. Skirts were slim with a gentle drape and worn with a neat, supple version of Prada's backpack. Spacious handbags that carried papers, files, and the paraphernalia of cosmetics and keys retained their popularity. But now they grew enormous, adorned with tassels, gilt studs, stitching, and a mix of textured leathers. Pockets held mobile phones, wallets, and so forth. Increasingly, the handbag made its own statement, its size and decoration giving it more significance than the wearer's clothes.

The great names in leather pursued a policy of glossy promotion and show biz endorsement. Fashionistas were persuaded to buy products favored by pop stars and footballers, their wives and girlfriends. Gossip pages were encouraged to show a rock musician or movie star carrying a luxury handbag with the logo clearly displayed.

RIGHT: There was a trend towards soft bags that fell comfortably against the body. This large pouch was designed for the high end of the market, and could be carried when wearing something formal, or if a casual look was required, the handles could hooked over the shoulder and the bag tucked under the arm.

LEFT: This is a "bling" bag, silver colored and showy. To keep your lipstick handy, there is a leather-covered cylinder attached to an external pouch and this holds a compact. This kind of important-looking statement handbag was favored throughout this decade.

RIGHT: The length of this handbag gives it the look of a saddlebag. The reptile markings are cleverly arranged, and the long chain handle confirms that it is meant to bring an elegant touch to the wardrobe. This was absolutely an accessory for a high flyer.

But another fashion influence came from the rock stars, Madonna and Britney Spears. These two women were not interested in old-time elegance or restraint. Both performed in glittering raunchy costumes that exhibited a lot of flesh. Versace made outrageous wardrobes for the entertainers and also designed handbags decorated with feathers, crystals, and sequins.

On the street, young women strolled about in velvet, lace, and satin, fabrics once restricted to evening wear. Underwear became outerwear as girls appeared in flimsy petticoat dresses and corsets or bustiers. These clothes were worn with machine-embroidered and beaded bags made in China, which added Oriental dash to the outfit. Reticules, easy to carry in clubs and at gigs, made a comeback. They sparkled with sequins, crystals, and glass beads.

LEFT: The label confirms that the handbag is made from real snakeskin. The initial excitement over synthetic fabrics had faded and now, discerning shoppers wanted the "real thing." The interior of this high-end handbag is fitted to a very high standard.

Jamin
Puech

Isabelle Puech and her husband Benoit Jamin opened a small boutique, Jamin Puech, in Paris in 1988. In her early years Isabelle traveled the world, and her sensibilities have been formed by the traditional crafts and patterns she absorbed as a child. Jamin Puech's decorative purses are hand-beaded and embroidered in curved designs of abstract plant forms. Craftsmen, working in small cottage workshops across France, do the delicate handwork, and total output is limited to 50,000 bags each year. The early collections preferred small, soft shapes in metallic leathers, satins, and furs. The subtle range of color and texture found an appreciative niche in the market. Jamin Puech's latest collections include bamboo and canvas, and tend towards a more structured shape than the 1990s output. Still, dreamy bohemians—those who need a gorgeously decorative handbag to express their personality—remain steady clients.

ABOVE: One of their earliest collections was called "Travels and life of a tattooed sailor." The title conveys the quality of their dreamy, romantic designs. The green confection resembles a rock pool, soft greens waved with foam around a cluster of smooth pebbles.

LEFT: Isabelle Puech and her husband, Benoit Jamin, are the creative force behind the Jamin Puech company. Both studied costume design before launching their handbag business.

LEFT: The artistic output of Jamin Puech is not confined to the soft or gentle. The abstract mix of circles and squares makes a handsome, abstract statement of great panache.

BELOW: This fringed handbag acknowledges the leatherworking skills and traditions of Native Americans. Much of their inspiration is drawn from cultures outside Europe.

HANDBAGS

The aim of Feminists to diminish the differences between the genders was ignored. Madonna showed women the power of their sexuality. Once again, the female body was curved and shaped by firm underwear. The Wonderbra promised a deep cleavage, essential when wearing a flimsy, theatrical outfit. Advertising became overtly sexual, as in the campaigns of Calvin Klein who sold his tailored shoulder bags through erotic images.

Julia Roberts in the film *Pretty Woman* also showed that the right clothes could transform any girl—even the escort she portrayed—into a conventional beauty. Meg Ryan in *When Harry Met Sally* represented another style. Her look was relaxed and off-beat, unconcerned with a high-end wardrobe. These various role models—ecologists, ambitious executives, singers, and movie stars—created a confused market making it difficult for designers to anticipate a fashion trend.

RIGHT: These extremely decorative purses were retailed in high street boutiques. They were made in China, and the beadwork is so pleasing that the bag neither dated nor defined its wearer as being part of a particular social group.

LEFT: This tiny disco bag fits neatly onto the wrist while the wearer dances. The bead decoration is whimsical, and the metal work refers to historical wrought iron work. The velvet handle ends in a soft round knob that obscures the clasp.

BELOW: When opened one facet of the four sides reveals an interior big enough for a lipstick, keys, a travel pass, and a credit card, but very little else. The purse was made in China.

LEFT: This gorgeous bag relies on startling color and clever cutting for maximum effect. Subtle stitching adds texture, and the handles can be adjusted to carry the handbag or use it as a shoulder bag. The design was intended for sale in top retail outlets.

Faced by this gaudy freedom, the Americans Ralph Lauren and Donna Karan concentrated on elegance. They designed pared-down wardrobes of well-cut pant suits, a draped jacket over straight pants, and narrow dresses. These were worn with purses as sleek and minimal as an attaché case. Long shoulder straps meant the bag rested against the upper thigh.

The retailer Gap sold this relaxed American style on main street. Blue jeans and khaki chinos were bought by both sexes. Tailored shirts and close-fitting T-shirts looked well with a neat backpack and once again, men began to carry bags. The rugged connotations of the backpack gave the Prada design credence with the male sex. After all, they needed bags for their gym and sports equipment. Young women carried shoppers with long handles.

LEFT: Soft, relaxed, unassuming, and capacious: this handbag suited the casual chic of American dressing. It could be carried to the stores or used for the office.

RIGHT: This early computer bag is made of a resilient synthetic material, closely resembling leather in its appearance. The zipped pocket on the front flap was designed to hold the booster plug, and the fabric handle is adjustable. Similar bags were soon available in markets and department stores.

Air travel was now commonplace and Vuitton revamped the Noë bag into a clever carry-on handbag with a transparent upper section sitting on a leather base. Everyone was traveling with a laptop computer, and bags appeared that would discreetly encase this essential item. Matching travel handbags, often with a strap hung across the body, accompanied the computer case. Crucially, the movie star Johnny Depp was photographed disembarking with his Fendi laptop case. Fendi also designed a large soft crushable duffel bag.

The market place was global, and the major names extended their outlets and their merchandise. They gave their name and logo to ready-to-wear couture, sunglasses, pens, scarves, perfumes, jewelry, and furnishings. Huge shopping malls opened up in Europe, Singapore, Sydney, Beijing, and Moscow. In these malls, Chanel, Ralph Lauren, Vuitton and similar names installed glamorous stores to feed the international market with luxury products.

RIGHT: This design is one of the most popular produced by Mulberry. Customers like the bold straps and buckles and, of course, the roomy interior.

RIGHT: This is the façade of the Bill Amberg shop in the prestigious London area of Notting Hill. Large glass windows are angled on a corner, and the interior is arranged in clean, minimalist lines that reflect the modernity of Amberg's leather designs.

Bill
Amberg

ABOVE: This portrait of Bill Amberg has captured the energy of this dedicated leather craftsman.

Even as a child growing up in Northamptonshire, England, Bill Amberg designed bags and wallets. He spent some time studying leathercraft at the Jam Factory in Adelaide, Australia. Here he learnt *cuir bouilli*, a method of boiling or soaking leather before molding it into shape. He opened his own workshop in London in 1983. Amberg constantly seeks innovative ways to handle leather. He explores the treatment, cutting, and folding of this fabric and his designs reflect his craftsman's appreciation of the material. His handbag designs are modern, with simple lines that are both beautiful and functional. Like other designers, Amberg has diversified, and he also makes leather floors and wall coverings. His handbag outlets are few, and his products are not only luxury items but are regarded as classic "heirloom" purchases.

RIGHT: This 2009 bag exemplifies his artistic use of leather. Textures are contrasted against each other, and there is also an interesting mix of two hues within one color.

239

RIGHT: Charles Jourdan made this handbag of dyed deer fur. As an exclusive craftsman and designer, he was not interested in the ever-changing fads of the high street market and this handbag is timeless in its design.

LEFT: Original in concept and expertly crafted, bags created by Janine Puech are—as are Charles Joudan's bags—beyond the merely fashionable. She prefers natural fibers and organic materials in her elaborate, decorative handbags, such as this adorable little pouch.

Models were turned into celebrities, worthy of imitation. Previously they were anonymous clotheshorses, but Naomi Campbell and Kate Moss, photographed endlessly, were now seen at parties and high-end restaurants, and their image set the standard for shoppers. Other women became celebrities simply by having their photograph appear frequently in the gossip magazines. All displayed brand handbags heavy with ornament.

There was a backlash, though. Grand establishments such as Hermès and Balenciaga resisted the urge to enter the huge consumer market and retained an image of exclusivity. There was a market for those who had the money to seek alternatives to the expensive but popular logo brands. The English leatherworker and designer, Bill Amberg, opened a workshop. His handcrafted purses of uncluttered design in rich, earthy colors gained a discerning clientele. Jamin Puech, a French handbag maker, started a line in sequined and small painted handbags. She used raffia, silk and ribbons to decorate her eccentric designs.

LEFT: These three women were among the most powerful leaders in the world of fashion, and they are dressed with all the shimmer of the decade. On the far left is Anna Wintour, holding a clutch, and beside her is Carolyn Roehmer. Both women are leading fashion editors. On the right is Donna Karan, founder of a major design house. They are at a fashion event, promoting the artistic creativity of clothing design.

Haute couture looked for ways to counteract the popular market. The development of the "fashion week" gave the designers an opportunity to assert their fashion supremacy. These events are held in Paris, London, New York, and Milan and are highly publicized, theatrical events of lights, dance, and music. The couture houses show off their clothes and accessories to movie stars, footballers' wives, politicians, fashion journalists, and celebrities. Fashion, as manufactured by the *haute couture* houses, was raised to an art form worthy of exhibitions held in the grandest museums, such as the Victoria and Albert in London or the Mode in Antwerp. In these ways, the exclusivity of certain brands was defined and lifted from the swarming retail market.

RIGHT: Two young women photographed in Tokyo prove the power of global marketing in the handbag world. The one on the left wears a handbag made in Burberry check, an English design that proved a winner in every country. The woman on the right wears a soft, pouchy bag, a look made popular by American manufacturers.

LEFT: Manufacturing output from China brought a massive economic change to the world of geo-politics, and western companies invested heavily in this country's growth. This handbag, in a neo Art Deco style, is purely western in its design references but it was made in China to sell in Europe and America.

Ralph
Lauren

The success of Ralph Lauren typifies the 1990s. His brand name is attached to clothes, accessories, and home furnishings, and all represent exclusivity and luxury. As a boy he used to make and sell ties to his schoolmates. He then went on to study business, working in retail before opening his own firm in 1972. He first sold his Polo shirts for men, and then moved into creating elegant clothing for both men and women. His purses are not revolutionary but are beautifully made. His Ricky handbag resembles a rail travel bag from the 1890s. It is sturdy with functional, not ornamental, clasps and buckles, and comes in patent leather, crocodile, and faux leopard skin. His Equestrian is a soft pouch patterned with images related to horse riding. In 1997 the Ralph Lauren company went public, and by 2007 his brand was being sold worldwide in luxury retail outlets.

RIGHT: The Ralph Lauren premises in New York occupy an historic, elegant but comfortable building. The interiors of his stores reflect these qualities, and are furnished in warm leathers, woods, and old-time photographs.

LEFT: Unmistakeably Ralph Lauren because of its minimal decoration and robust elegance, this firm hold-all makes an enviable travel companion. He designs for the relaxed but confident dresser.

Despite these attempts to retain an elite label, expensive purses were quickly copied in China and sold through an ever-increasing number of down-market retail outlets in the West. The logos of the great houses were copied on "rip-off" handbags and numerous legal actions were taken against infringements of trademark copyrights.

The credit card shopping of the 1980s continued, but there was a growing murmur of dissent. Ecological concerns, such as those expressed by Rachel Carson in the 1970s, became widespread. People believed manufacture, with its excessive use of the Earth's resources, could severely damage the planet. In response to these concerns, scientists began to explore man-made regenerated fibers.

RIGHT: Emily Jo Gibbs made this shopper of basket weave. The polished metal flowers on the lid are a reminder of the natural plants used to make the straw of the base. The handbag is a symbolic approval, perhaps, of organic eco-friendly products.

Handbags assumed a crafted rather than a machine-made look. Nathalie Hambro designed wrought-metal bags, even crochet bags made a reappearance, and the Australian Belinda Gunn concocted net bags with handles of beads strung together in a down-home way. The handbags of the British designer, Emily Jo Gibbs, can be described as works of art. Gold thread and seashells trail over a silk surface, or exquisitely embroidered birds perch on tasseled frames. Although her work is snapped up by museums, the handbags are practical and functional.

But the majority of designers appreciated synthetic materials resembling leopard's fur, zebra skin, jungle camouflage, or indeed any pattern a customer wanted on their handbag. This overwhelmed any concern about manufacturing methods. And fashion was big business. High street stores opened that sold only purses, while there was a big enough market to sustain the low-end specialist boutiques. There was a choice of cheap, hand-embroidered clutches, huge over-decorated pouches, and crafted bags which sold for large sums.

LEFT: These handbags have been reported as practical and functional, but Emily Jo Gibbs's work has been bought into museum collections as "art and craft" pieces. Certainly, these metal structures resemble small sculptural works more than handbags.
Fashion writers have described them as jewel-like, the perfect adornment to the little black dress.

LEFT: The zipper has a neat, well crafted tag with the Dior logo clearly stamped.

BELOW: Christian Dior designed this wonderful handbag of dyed fur, catching both high chic and a carefree, colorful high street style. The color combination and the partially beaded handle bring it a bright contemporary look, but the purse is carefully and meticulously crafted.

In the 1990s materials were highly developed. They could be stretched, molded, patterned, and colored in many ways and the demand was high among enthusiastic shoppers for ever-more interesting handbag designs.

BELOW: The interior has a leather label confirming the maker of the bag. Even in a crowded market, Christian Dior is probably the most famous haut couture house in the world, and the company supplies their products to selected retailers.

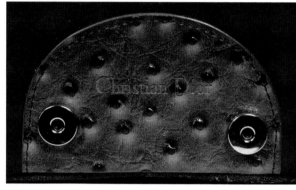
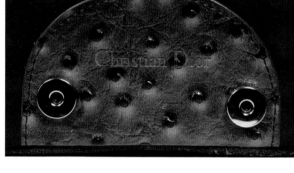

RIGHT: The high street department stores and boutiques offer the average woman a huge choice of design, color, and shape. Here faux leopard skin snuggles against a gaudy display of flowers. Both designs adorn handbags. Complex technology has made an extraordinary variety of handbags available to the majority of women.

2000s
CRAFT AND CONSUMER

I t is difficult to identify fashion trends or leaders in this decade. The choice of handbags is enormous in its variety, and we are reminded of the 1970s mantra: "Fashionable people are all right but they are not a mass market." And, perhaps, in the 2000s, fashion finally, became fully democratized, a process started so long ago by the '50s designer, McCardell, and made inevitable by advancing technology.

RIGHT: Press photographers besiege the uber-fashionista, Paris Hilton, and consequently her image and her gorgeous purse will be seen by millions of women. In the 2000s, handbag manufacturers relied on this kind of celebrity endorsement to give their products status and high sales.

Major designers, once so exclusive, agreed to franchise contracts with high street retailers, thus exploiting brand recognition at every level of the market. Madonna, the rock musician and actress, uses her name on designs for a mid-market fashion store. A footballer's wife starts her own fashion house on the strength of her celebrity name. But no one celebrity predominates as a style icon. Haut couture no longer reigns over fashion. Women seem immune to advice from fashion writers or the displays at fashion weeks.

RIGHT: When a collection, developed by the celebrity Madonna, was opened at a high street retailer, mobs of women stormed the shop. An assistant (right in picture) wears a T-shirt emblazoned with a giant M, the logo for designs by Madonna.

LEFT: Victoria Beckham lays claim to the field by placing her handbag on the turf. She stole the spotlight from her soccer-king husband, David Beckham, at his inauguration into the MLS team in California. Fashionistas know there is little that can compete against the glory of a pink Hermès bag.

These assumptions are strengthened by the work of the blogger, The Sartorialist (real name Scott Schuman). He specializes in photos of mostly anonymous people on the street. A glance at his work shows a New Yorker in a short flared skirt and white sandals, carrying a black patent 1890-style luggage handbag. Or look at a woman in a Milan street. She wears red leggings, a silver lamé T-shirt and brandishes a clutch made of long white fur. Here is a young woman in a petticoat dress with a striped raffia woven shopper, while a tartan-skirted girl in Brazil carries a clear orange, structured leather handbag. Elsewhere a woman in black leather hangs a linen tote from her shoulder.

LEFT: It is a universally acknowledged truth that a girl carries her life in her handbag but popping a pet among the letters, lipstick, diary, and keys was unusual. This "doggy bag" was spotted in Beijing, China. When celebrities took to carrying lapdogs everywhere, manufacturers were quick to respond, producing dinky little carry bags designed to accommodate tiny animals. Vuitton was the first into the field but others soon followed.

RIGHT: The Sartorialist who had fun taking photos of stylish strangers, is himself caught on camera. He looks suspiciously like a man who hates to have the camera turned on himself.

Even the editor of *Vogue* would be stumped if asked to find a common trend in fashion from these contemporary images yet The Sartorialist has been voted among the one hundred most influential men in fashion. It seems the unexpected personal statements he finds on the street serve as inspiration for designers.

Karl Lagerfield at Chanel uses polyethylene, aluminum, and tweed to shape a smooth abstract of a woman's body, curving comfortably on the wearer's hip. Prada makes long, deep bags hanging as low as the knee.

RIGHT: Karl Lagerfield was a daring innovator at the House of Chanel. This is a grand, bling version of the classic quilted bag, and has a large Chanel logo stitched on it's surface.

Celebrity magazines show uber fashionistas carrying puffed, padded handbags with wide, soft handles from Chanel. But some are carrying a Dolce and Gabbana structured bag, the leather cut and laid in scales against a firm surface fitted on a metal mount and carried on short handles. In the evening, big clutches are favored, held in the hand rather than tucked under the arm. These come in green crocodile skin, with a jeweled clasp. A crystal-covered rectangle of gilt, narrow but long, from Anya Hindmarch and gold, patterned leather from Luella are equally fashionable. There are no rules. Established leather houses, such as Coach in the U.S. keep their confidence in elegance and do not sway with fashion.

LEFT: The old string shopping bag has been transformed by Karl Lagerfield of Chanel. Beads, chains, and faux buckles make the dull traditional version into a charming beach bag. The designer matched it to the model's outfit for the 2010 Spring/Summer fashion show in Paris.

But the heavy decoration of the 1990s vanishes as the 2000s advance. A clean, uncluttered line emerges and is expressed in the work of Kate Spade. This American designer makes bright red totes, or patterns them with black and white polka dots. She creates saddlebags with minimum decoration. Her style is chic and practical.

LEFT: In the 2000s, synthetics aroused a certain disdain among some consumers. However, Prada was interested in the hardiness of synthetic fibers, and exploited them. This shopper in a light, resilient fabric overcame any vestiges of snobbery towards the "faux."

RIGHT: Audrina Patridge, TV and movie star, accentuates her brilliant yellow Prada clutch by carrying it against an outfit of slate grays and black. The paparazzi snapped her when she went to the hit 3-D movie, *Avatar*, in Hollywood, California.

Falchi's handbags are fringed and covered in fat, leather flowers. Balenciaga enlivens the handbag world with his motorcycle-inspired handbags, especially his Lariat design.

RIGHT: This handbag has the distressed air so liked by the boho-chic tribe. It is Balenciaga's Giant Versace, and its squashy shape and external purse guaranteed its popularity.

Silvia Fendi designs a long roll, slightly squashy and very friendly. She calls it the Baguette. This is an instant success. Fendi uses leather and straw; or velvet and embroidered silk, or fur and snakeskin to ring changes on editions of the Baguette. Women love every one of them, delighting in a femininity lacking in the functional appearance of the latest Ralph Lauren and Mulberry bags.

LEFT: One of the most popular bags of the decade came from Fendi. This is a demure black leather variation of the Baguette, but Fendi satisfied a wide range of tastes and also produced this handbag in florals, stripes and the like.

HANDBAGS

On the high street, textile bags, rich with appliqué work, or embroidery, sequins, and beads, are popular. These come close to the Baguette in concept, but some are gathered into a decorative mount, others are bags of suede or soft leather. Bags smothered with intricate bead embroidery are so pretty, they are worn day or night. Patterns hark back to Art Deco, Art Nouveau, and the Orient.

Satchel bags and totes remain popular with big brand names and the high street, encouraging the British firm, Burberry, traditionally a clothing manufacturer, to launch a high-end purse collection. The most popular buys in the mass market are small satchels, often of moc-croc with exterior pockets and numerous buckles. The straps are adjustable and can be carried or hung from the shoulder. Designer's work is copied but, where the master uses suede, the imitation may be of bright pink nylon netting.

RIGHT: The world of easy purchase and great choice is proved in the astonishing variety of handbags displayed in this high street boutique. Craftsmanship is not a priority for customers here, but they hope to find style and hot trends in this kind of retailer.

The global economy takes a downturn and desperate to sell high cost purses, the pop-up shop is introduced—a department store gives temporary space to stalls, arranged as if they were in a self-contained store. Promotions of special discounts and the like are offered to shoppers who can buy prêt-a-porter products from DKNY, Chanel, Ralph Lauren, Moschino, and other logo brands. The American, Michael Kors retails his handbags in collection boutiques throughout the world.

LEFT: A high-end retailer displays their choice of handbags in a pop-up shop. These temporary outlets are designed to allow the concentrated promotion and large sales of a particular brand.

Anya
Hindmarch

Anya Hindmarch (1968–), born in England, was inspired by Italian design and architecture. After learning to produce her own bags, nineteen-year old Hindmarch opened a small shop in Walton Street, London in 1987. By 2009 the Anya Hindmarch business had grown to fifty-four stores around the world. Alongside opening new stores, Anya Hindmarch has developed an exclusive range of Hampers for Selfridges and designed a limited edition collection for Target stores in the United States. Anya Hindmarch bags continue to be celebrity favorites, worn by everyone from Reese Witherspoon and Claudia Schiffer to Jourdan Dunn.

As Lisa Armstrong, Fashion Editor of *The Times*, commented: "Anya has demonstrated consistent ability to come up with a slick must-have bag every season—no mean feat in a market dominated by much bigger brands. Her energy and imaginative marketing are outstanding and are on the way to making her an international name."

A talented and successful designer, Hindmarch is very public in the promotion of ecological and charitable concerns.

ABOVE: Portrait of Anya Hindmarch.

RIGHT: This evening clutch, along with striped storage bag, represents an assured, tasteful accessory.

LEFT: In a short space of time, Anya Hindmarch has moved a small handbag workshop into a global business. Her London shop window is a statement of wealth and luxury.

There is a serious mood in the first decade of the millennium. No one can be immune to the gulf between the wealthy West and the economic struggles of the peoples of Africa and Asia. Nor can the poverty in the West be ignored. And now, the ecology of the planet is of widespread concern. Philanthropy colors the huge profits made by the corporations.

Ralph Lauren advises his customers that when they purchase a certain purse, some of its profits are paid to charity. He is not alone. Bill Amberg gives a percentage of sales to medical research; the pen maker, Mont Blanc, donates to literacy programs in the third world. Many brands donate to a variety of charities. Stella McCartney promotes animal welfare, so her bags are never made of leather.

Anya Hindmarch offers part of the profits from a selection of her bags to the American Red Cross and numerous other charitable organizations. Her shopper carrying the words "I am not a plastic bag" is a famous contribution to the ecology movement, and the idea has been copied many times.

LEFT: Consumers of the 2000s are concerned about the ecological effects of throwaway plastic and metal cans. In response, manufacturers began to recycle the rubbished material to make woven purses. Cans were also recycled as decorative elements on handbags. These examples are displayed in a makeshift showroom in Manila, Philippines.

RIGHT: The craze for eco-friendly products produced a hostility towards throw-away plastic shopping bags. These recyclable shoppers, clearly announcing their green credentials, attracted queues of eager purchasers. Plastic lost its popularity in the 2000s because it is not bio-degradable and many fear plastic shopping bags will litter Planet Earth for generations to come.

There is a return to "retro" clothing, and fashion writers urge the rich not be wasteful, but buy second-hand, preferably stylish, scarce numbers from the 1940s and 1960s. The charity organization, Oxfam, plans a fashion show of logo brands or re-vamped, "customized" versions of the clothes handed in at their second-hand clothes shops.

High street retailers respond with "retro style" purses, plausible imitations of patent leather '40s with a gilt clasp, or a patchwork '60s clutch. These goods are a lot cheaper than the bags found in genuine retro outlets. Down-market retailers, such as Target (USA) and Primark (UK), attract thousands of shoppers who are delighted to buy plastic lookalikes of designer bags or faux retro items, even if the quality is not high.

LEFT: Manufacturers moved their operations to China, where labor was cheaper than in the West and because computer technology allowed vast production output with little skill required. This is a view of the handbag selection at a successful high street retailer in Britain, and the number and variety of purses is staggering. No one needs to go without the latest design and at a price any citizen can afford.

ABOVE: The leather maker, Dean, in California represents a different business ideal from that of the huge factory production favored by major manufacturers. Bean recycles leather, has limited output and creates easy, stylish bags of muted colors. This lovely design has a huge bangle handle, but also, straps for wearing the bag on the shoulder.

The decade draws to an end in a global financial recession. The rich, hinting at ecological correctness, search for goods made only from natural products —leather, silk, linen, fur, bamboo, and wood. Valentino Garavani bedecks an evening bag with ostrich feathers. Others use plain silk, adding interest with decorative clasps and mounts. Leather shoulder satchels make a comeback, with thick straps that sit comfortably, and can be adjusted to handles to be carried. Ostentatious decoration is quietly abandoned, and handbags assume a more austere appearance.

The vanity case returns. The cosmetic company, Crème de la Mer, commissions the leather workers, Globe-Trotter, to produce a limited edition of an immaculate silvered leather vanity case à la Arden. Shopping bags, with a logo or an ecological message flourished across them, are everywhere.

LEFT: The original handbag backpack was small and neat, but it has grown into a large hold-all to carry anything from lipstick to sports equipment. It is used by both sexes. This shows a design from the British master craftsman, Bill Amberg.

RIGHT: Security controls at airports grew very strict in the 2000s and women were not allowed to carry both a handbag and a cabin bag on board. Jean Paul Gaultier of Hermès designed this large portmanteau to fulfill the new travel regulations. It has the elegance of a handbag but is big enough to store the requirements for a long haul journey or a weekend away.

RIGHT: This handbag comes from the craftsmen at Coach Leatherworks, whose headquarters are in New York. This company has a high reputation for quality production and a distinctive American style: chic, tailored, yet relaxed. Started in a loft in Manhattan in 1941, Coach operates in over twenty countries and has major workshops in Asia.

Not all is democratized or lost to mass production. Kelly bags are customized for the personal shopper; Anya Hindmarch and Bill Amberg take commissions from individuals. The House of Delvaux continues to follow its craft methods, producing few but special runs of its purses. The prestigious leather house of Coach and Dooney and Bourke maintain high standards in the American market, and continue to craft satchels and dignified handbags.

During the London Fashion Week of 2009, the pundits are surprised by the success of Jaeger. This company, perceived as ultra conventional in its approach, shows an exciting range of handbags. These are big, practical, and bold in color. For instance, Brittania comes in pillar-box red, and the aquamarine Stanton has a zipped base and double handles so the bag can be carried by hand or worn on the shoulder. Chloe is admired for her robust designs, recalling mini suitcases, with exterior pockets and spacious interiors. She uses saddle stitching and gilt links as ornament.

LEFT: The big, shiny statement handbag did not disappear in the 2000s. The Chloe (left) became an instant "It" bag that every serious fashionista had to own. The shiny surface gives due warning of its bold nature.

RIGHT: Rock stars, celebrities, and the wives of eminent men became designers, relying on their famous names to sell the goods. This sturdy rectangular handbag comes from the Paris Hilton workshop, and her name is used repetitively across its surface. The glittering heart ornament typifies Ms Hilton's style.

The major houses concentrate on useful, big bags in response to the market. Modern women admire style, but they need a useful handbag that carries the essential components of a varied life. Vuitton's totes, despite a casual appearance, have firm closures and are chic in design. This house represents Marni who makes exciting handbags of soft leather, with unusual mounts, and straps threaded through acrylic bangle handles. The Burberry Hobo Nova follows this "big bag" vogue: it is neat, deep, and comes in the much-loved Burberry check.

LEFT: Long ago Burberry created a plaid, or tartan pattern, but did they anticipate the public response? Women loved the design and could not have enough of it. This is the Burberry Hobo Nova, a closed shopper in the much-loved plaid.

Logos are not as glaringly obvious as they had been at the end of the twentieth century. Marc Jacobs uses a quiet label to identify his handbags and Vuitton continues to use the repeat pattern of their logo, now as much part of their products as their superb craftsmanship.

BELOW: Brash brassy logo displays lost their allure during this decade. This elegant leather handbag comes from a major house, but Marc Jacobs chose to keep their identity discrete. A small label identifies the product.

LEFT: Vuitton clung to a proud history in leatherwork but, finally, in keeping with modernity, embraced high-tech fabrics. Their handbag of silvers and shiny blues, shown here, set a trend, and is, of course, beautifully crafted. The design sets a trend and many silvery copies of poorer quality appeared on the market.

The handbag market has become a very important part of the fashion business, and while this gives manufacturers great sales, it allows for new young craftsmen to set up workshops. The Californian company, Dean recycles coat leather in their bags, and delight in subtle colors of sludge greens and grays. They don't line their bags but their products are so well made, they simply distress into beautiful age and do not fall apart. All these young designers are aware that quality is of prime importance to their buyers.

Whether she can buy the best or only a copy, every woman is glad the skills of master craftsmen have not been lost to the computerized manufacture of handbags. And glad, too, that the great designers continue to create beautiful handbags that inspire imitation.

LEFT: The prestigious name, Dior, is wrapped boldly round these clutches, and this not only advertises the brand but confirms the wearer's high economic status. But this display is from the Counterfeit Museum, in France. Here the museum shows both genuine and fake handbags to educate and help the public recognize the differences, and so avoid fraudulent purchases.

RIGHT: Vuitton has never seen any need to alter their traditional cover of the repeated logo that appears on their products. It has appeared in various colors, but the much-loved and distinctive favorite is used on this, the Batignolle bag.

Balenciaga

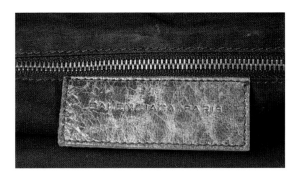

LEFT: The exclusive trademark label is stitched into the finely lined interior.

BELOW: The new products from the Balenciaga label maintain the high standards implied by the great designer's name. On this bag the color is warm, as Balenciaga preferred, and the stitching details reassuring. Zips and metal rivets are incorporated into the design.

This story is one that reflects the turn of the century, of corporate marketing set against craftsmen and couturists. Cristobal Balenciaga opened a couture house in Spain but fled to Paris during the Spanish Civil War. He was soon famous: Balenciaga gave the world the tunic dress, the chemise dress, and the sack. He closed in 1968, and died in 1972. During the '80s when the acquisition of rights to reputable designer names was a major business strategy, Gucci bought the Balenciaga label. In 1992, Josephus Melchior Thimister became house designer. He developed a specialist line in handbags soon recognised for its interesting design and high quality.

Balenciaga handbags in the 2000s earned a reputation for beautiful simplicity, influencing other designers. They are sold in select boutiques but sales rely on the old, famous name and are not promoted as part of the Gucci empire.

LEFT: Christobel Balenciaga admires the kitchen-ware while walking with the American fashion editor of *Harper's Bazaar* and writer Carmel Snow, in December 1952 in New York.

LEFT: Marie Osmond, the country music artist, is seen with the handbags that are part of her Marie's Lifestyle Collection of Accessories. She donated some of her profits to a charity. Her colorful bags, in fabrics that hint at Persian and Oriental pattern motifs, reflect her own warm personality and are not designed for conservative tastes.

LEFT: The term "bohemian" implies an artistic, free spirit and, in fashion terms, "boho-chic" describes an artfully careless appearance. This handbag uses an unusual color combination, and threads colorful elastic straps through a chunky chain attachment. Deliberately, it tries to look un-contrived and spontaneous. The handbag comes from the house of Proenzer Schouler, New York.

LEFT: The pop group, Girls Aloud, line up for the Brit Awards, a media event held in 2009. It is clear there is no common fashion silhouette followed by the group, but a range of styles, all acceptable. In the center, Nicola Roberts wears a frock reflecting a line fashionable early in the twentieth century, and her shimmering clutch continues the theme.

RIGHT: In the first decade of the twenty-first century, women showed nostalgia for past styles, or retro fashion. This pleated satin clutch with a glittering bow decoration is reminiscent of Art Deco and the 1930s. Carla Bruni-Sarkozy, wife of the French president, chose to carry it to an evening occasion held for NATO leaders.

LEFT: Prancing before the adoring cameras, Eva Herzigova, a celebrity model, shows off her fringed cocktail dress. But she understands the fashion importance of the handbag, and brandishes her large clutch for the photographers.

LEFT: Gucci's Hysteria followed the market's preference for soft, casual, and easy style. The subtle color and the gathering give the bag all the best style motifs of the last years' of the decade.

RIGHT: This designer has used a radical mix of textures. The hard line of the clutch handle is repeated in the design motif of straight, sequined lines. These frame an embroidered image, but the rest of the bag is covered in an intricate web of crystals. The total effect is wild and glamorous.

LEFT: So eclectic and individual was 2000s fashion, that this pantomime outfit raised few eyebrows. Bridget Marquardt, a TV actor, wore it when she attended a media event, where the dress was deemed acceptable, if exhibitionist. Her handbag is a fluffy concoction of pastel colored loops and curlicues.

Kate
Spade

Kate Brosnahan from Missouri was not trained as a leather worker or a designer. She worked as a fashion writer on *Mademoiselle* magazine in New York, then in fashion retail where she met her husband, Andy Spade. In 1993, she launched her version of the Prada backpack. Kate Spade did not use black nylon, but created a girlie box lined with gingham. Her work is not radical, but relies on classic shapes made in clear, bright, color and enhanced with a cute bow or border. The style suits the sober, sensible mood of the 2000s and the Kate Spade brand was very successful in a very short time. During the 2000s, it was sold in outlets across the USA and the Far East. The company was bought by the Nieman Marcus Group but is now owned by Liz Claiborne and has an annual turnover of millions.

LEFT: These models represent the Kate Spade style: young, fresh, fashionable and colorful. Her designs are very popular in the USA, and the photograph shows a lovely variety of glitzy totes and sharp little clutches.

LEFT: Kate and her husband, Andy Spade were both familiar with the retail world, and together they harnessed their skills in marketing. Kate's love and knowledge of fashion persuaded the couple to launch into purse manufacturing. The combination of artistic creativity and business acumen helped establish quickly their company in a competitive market.

LEFT: Computer technology has expanded methods of printing fabrics and textiles, allowing ways of reproducing images and designs undreamt of in earlier decades. This clutch has reproduced photographs of the movie star, Omar Sharif, and the Lebanese actress, Cyrine Abdel Nour, chose to carry it after she starred in a film with Sharif.

LEFT: Bucking the trend of making the handbag an important statement, this clutch has been chosen because it is as unobtrusive as possible. It is small, carries little embellishment and is color-toned to match the wearer's outfit.

293

RIGHT: This evening clutch refers to Art Deco, the ever-popular artistic style. The smooth enameled surface and rhinestone decoration are perfect replicas of this retro look. A heavy finger ring complements the design.

LEFT: During the 2000s, were shoppers demanding nostalgia, or were designers digging into the past for ideas and selling the sentiment? This textile bag is the grandchild of the crocheted wool bags made during the 1940s—but with an ironic difference. This gorgeous modern bag is woven with gold thread, and its Indian designer has aimed the product at a very small, wealthy, and elite market.

RIGHT: Jimmy Choo borrowed ornaments from the twentieth century Punk movement, and used studs and zips to adorn this black leather clutch. But, unlike Punk decoration, Choo's design has a subtle and pleasing symmetry.

LEFT: Erin Cummings, a successful TV actress, attends a premiere in California. Her only jewelery is a dull, heavy bangle and a clutch that is encrusted with colored crystals and sequins.

RIGHT: The knots and loops, the gathered contours of this reptile skin bag are characteristic of Falchi. He was intrigued by the dying of leather and by the folding and manipulation of this natural fabric.

RIGHT: The red Dior bag shows trend details that could be found in most handbag designs of this decade, despite the wide-ranging tastes of women shoppers. Chain handles and fancy clasps were popular at haut couture and high street levels, as were exposed logos. Here, Dior uses all three elements—the logo, a large metallic D, is attached to the links of the chain and the clasp is an eye-catching metallic button.

Novelty Bags
Fun Statements

The handbag maker, Anne Marie of France, broke the aesthetic rules set by the design writer, Edward de Bono, who believed the shape of an object should indicate the purpose of that object. So, following his dictates, an umbrella stand should not look like a teapot. Anne Marie specialized in purses resembling clocks, telephones, drums, writing desks, and all manner of other things. And Katherine Baumann created a bag that was a glittering model of the liner *Titanic*.

LEFT: Ninteenth century travelers were excited by images on handbags that showed off their foreign journey, but can these compare with models of tourist sites? Who could resist this mad little bag of a blue and brass Eiffel Tower, jauntily swinging on a velvet strap?

BELOW: The movie of the *Titanic* disaster persuaded shoppers to buy this model of the doomed ship if they could meet the price of this jeweled handbag from Kathrine Baumann.

©KBBH

At the turn of the twentieth century, English and American travelers to Europe returned carrying handbags decorated with views of a foreign city, or Mediterranean boats. In the 1950s, the vanity case, with its flat surfaces, was perfect for depicting pictures and messages. Palm trees from Hawaii, or cowboys in Texas, or the Eiffel Tower for Paris illustrated these vanity cases.

RIGHT: A collection of Kathrine Baumann's glittering novelty purses, designed to honor American consumer icons. Actually, these products have world-wide significance and need no description.

©McDonal's

©Coca-Cola

©KBBH

Lulu Guinness

Lulu Guinness launched her company in 1989. Wild praise in the fashion media paved the way for Lulu Guinness shops in London, New York, and Tokyo. Her creations are also sold in department and specialty stores including Harrods and Selfridges in the UK, Bergdof Goodman in New York, Le Bon Marché in Paris, and Lane Crawford in Hong Kong. There are also boutiques in New York, Tokyo, Osaka, and Fukuoka.

Lulu's collectable bags have been described as "tomorrow's treasures" and have become permanent fixtures in many museums. They have also been the subjects of two exhibitions in Sotheby's London and New York. Her bags are seen on the arms of celebrities, such as Dita von Tees, Sophie Dahl, and Keira Knightley.

Despite her success Lulu has never had any formal design training apart from a year's foundation course at art school and a long-standing passion for design and fashion. Lulu's strong personal style and her original ideas have played a large part in her success with her design inspiration springing partly from retro glamour and partly from modern chic.

LEFT: Guinness made a handbag that paid homage to an Art Deco Florida hotel, the Delano; it was so popular she made others in homage to the generic image of home. Her birdcage is a work of art.

ABOVE: The Lulu Guinness shop in London, England is depicted on the side of this bag.

RIGHT: Her window dressing showing row upon row of her "lips" handbags reveals the Guinness sense of fun and wit. This is her shop in London, England.

BELOW: The first flight across the Atlantic Ocean, made by the heroic American, Charles A.Lindberg inspired this fat little aeroplane handbag. Marked with the brave pilot's name, it was designed in Germany.

A handbag can make all sorts of witty statements. In 1984, Jean Charles de Castelbajac made a bag shaped like a huge glove. Katie Baumann specializes in glittering creations of popular consumer goods. She reproduced the Coca-Cola bottle as a purse, and also a hot dog, complete with tomato sauce. Both were made with crystals, glass beads, and rhinestones. Similar fun bags can be found in high street shops, albeit fashioned from printed plastic or fabric. What humor would be lost to us if designers stuck to Mr de Bono's rule?

When amazing inventions were introduced to the world, designers emerged with handbags representing the latest wonder. During the first quarter of the twentieth century there were many opportunities for these flights of fancy. Bag makers produced automobiles, planes, and telephones shaped from leather or cloth. A red patent leather bag shaped like a telephone was made by Dallas Handbags in the 1970s. Actually, it was more than a handbag: it was wired to be plugged in, and could make calls!

LEFT: The flowers-in-a-basket bag was conceived, first, by Schiaparelli who made a small soft bouquet of velvet and satin pansies for an evening bag. Her delightful concept has been frequently copied. This bold bucket of rich velvet roses is definitely a "statement" handbag and was made in the 2000s by Lulu Guinness.

BELOW: The red patent leather telephone is a handbag, but it is also a functioning telephone. The owner simply plugged her handbag to a power source to warn her date she might be late. Was this the first commercial mobile phone? This shiny and ingenious contraption came from the Dallas Company in the 1970s.

Moschino and Lulu Guinness in the 2000s have created much-loved humorous bags. Lulu Guinness creates a bouquet of flowers, or a Miami Hotel, or rows of little houses, and all are charmingly detailed with beads, embroidery, and appliqué.

Technology allows the designer such a delightful choice of material, color, and pattern, it is no surprise that crazy, funny, and amusing handbags are created for our pleasure.

RIGHT: Adorable Minnie Mouse is given the glamorous treatment she deserves. The artist in Kathrine Baumann inspired this gorgeous and witty homage to the little comic heroine.

©Disney

Kathrine
Baumann

Kathrine Baumann was a beauty queen, then a television actress in Los Angeles, before an accident left her scarred. Undeterred, she turned her artistic talents to purse design. She believes in glamour, and creates minaudières of exquisite craftsmanship. Kathrine follows an American aesthetic, her work reflecting the Pop Art of Andy Warhol. Her editions include Minnie Mouse, Miss Piggy, and Campbell's Soup. Each is made of brass—some lined with gold—and the details are patterned from precious stones and Zwarovski crystals. Her studios have perfected an unassailable method of attaching jewels to metal. She makes limited editions of each design, and movie stars attending the Oscars ceremony fight to carry a Kathrine Baumann. Her designs include soft pouches with highly decorative handles that can be detached and worn as a bracelet or a necklace. Artisans in California and Italy are employed to craft these gorgeous handbags.

RIGHT: Coca Cola has become a symbol of the USA, and Baumann elevates its famous soda can into a finely crafted purse. It is no surprise that she is seen as the Andy Warhol of the jewelery-designer world. She appreciates the significance of modern culture and gives it great value.

RIGHT: The Barbie Doll is essentially American but she has a global personality. Baumann's jeweled creations acknowledge the universal glamour of Barbie in these precious interpretations of the character and her accessories.

©Coca-Cola

©KBBH

©Mattel

A Visit to
Bill Amberg's
Workshop

Perhaps the engravings of old history books fix, within our minds, the image of a workshop, the master craftsman strolling about as some apprentices sit, working at a long table, while others bend over machines lined up in a row.

Walking into Bill Amberg's workshop, there is first, the warm aroma of leather followed by a sense of chaos. To one side, a shelving unit stands tall (left), filled with roll upon roll of leathers in a wonderful array of colors. Lengths of leather hang from pegs on the wall and squat machines lurk in unexpected places. Youths wander about doing their own thing; girls sit cross-legged, sorting through brass fittings. A man barks into a phone, while stabbing at a computer.

Of course, it is not chaos, but has the invisible order of artistic discipline.

A current of energy runs through the workshop, giving everyone a mutual sense of creative achievement with the shared ambition to make beautiful leather objects.

Steps in bag-making

A handbag is born through a series of sketches, refined until all the details are determined. The final drawing will show whether corners are curved or angular; it will specify the kinds of folding and stitching, how the zip or clasp will fit, if the handles will be joined with links, riveted onto the bag, or stitched in place.

The drawing is analyzed and broken down into measured sections, and pattern pieces are made. These are drawn onto a thick but not rigid cardboard that are then cut out. Leather is selected carefully—soft, rigid, ostrich skin, pony skin—the choice of texture and color is an integral part of the design.

The tools of the trade (right) are simple and traditional: knives, measuring instruments, hammers, brushes, and the like. The wooden rods are traditional tools used to neaten or give a decorative finish to folded joins of a leather product or alternatively, a modern hot crease electrical tool is employed. (This is not shown in this image.)

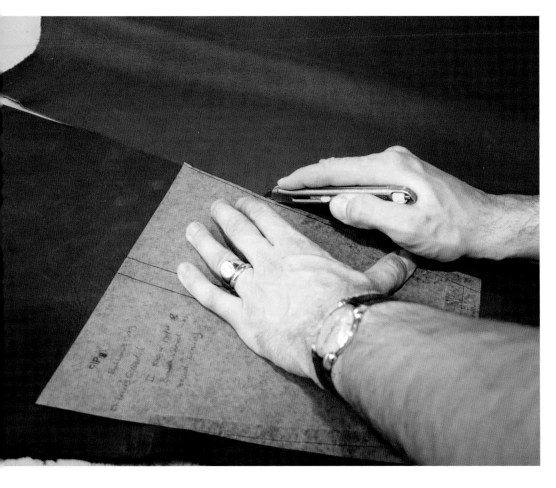

Most leather is thick and heavy. This machine splits the leather (below). The piece of leather is cut horizontally, through its depth, so that at the end of the splitting, there are two pieces of leather.

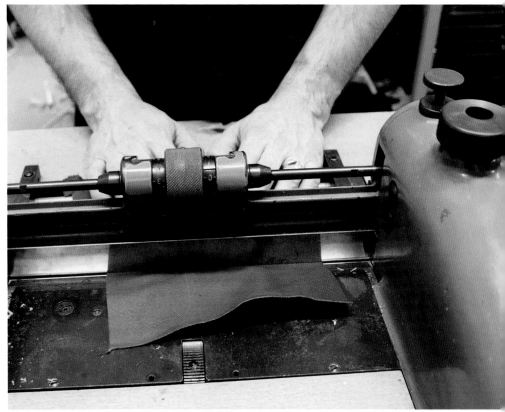

Each cardboard pattern piece (above) is pressed onto the leather and the craftsman holds this firm and unmoving, while the he cuts round the card using a craft knife.

The two pieces produced after splitting (left).
The smooth upper piece is selected, while the
lower piece is rejected.

Even split leather is thick and when two pieces are stitched together (left), they form a clumsy, ungainly seam. To avoid this, the edges of the pattern piece are put through a machine that shaves the underside, taking off a strip, about one inch wide, along the edge. This thinning of edges means that leather pattern pieces can be attached smoothly together. The thinning process is called skiving.

The bristles are thick and firm on the glue brush. Glue is painted along the skived strip (right) and the craftsman is careful not to let glue spread beyond this edge.

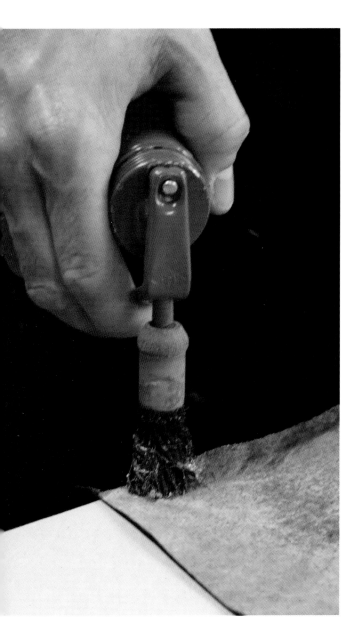

The pattern pieces may be joined along the glued skived margins, and the craftsman bangs a hammer firmly along the edges (below) to ensure the glue holds the pieces securely.

The design may require folding detail. The glued margin of one pattern piece is folded, and right side up, glued against the right side of the second piece and, again the join is secured by hammering along its length (below).

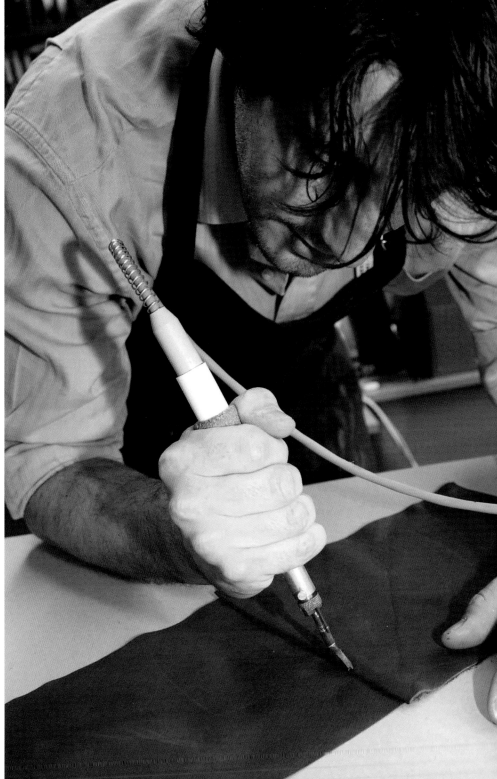

This step is not essential, but the bag design may demand a smoothed, tight fold as part of its decorative plan. If so, the fold at the join is hot creased (left). This creates a flat, distinctive line.

Depending on the design of the bag, the joins may be sewn after they have been glued (right). The machine has the appearance of a conventional sewing machine, but is modified to cope with the demands of leather. Most kinds of thread can be used—polyester, linen, cotton—and as shown here, it may contrast with the color of the leather.

In leather craft, the term "stitched" is used only for hand stitching, not machine sewing.

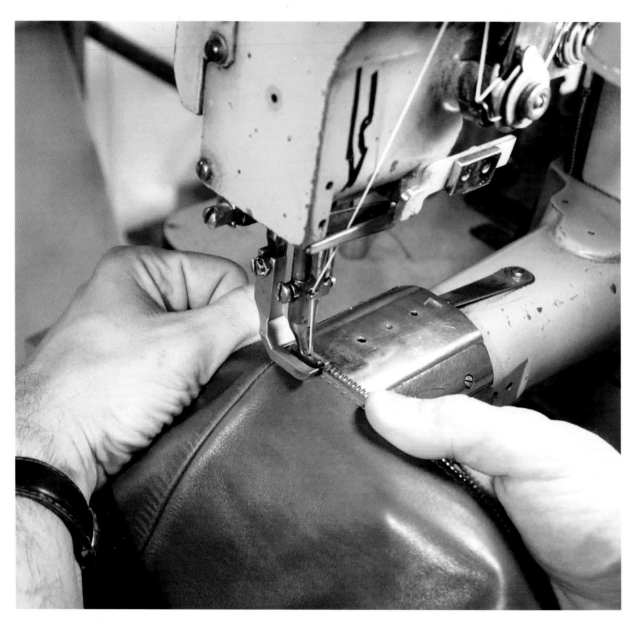

The joined pieces of the bag are flattened so the interior lining and any inner or outer pockets can be fitted. The links to hold the handle are attached. The flattened bag is folded and the final seams fixed together. At last, as shown here (left), the zip is sewn into place. (Sometimes it is glued.) The closing mechanism, whether zip or clasp, and the handles are the last details to be completed.

The finished article is soft and in the classic travel bag style (right). The outer lengths of the zip closing are threaded through buckles on each side, and the handles have been riveted into place.

Simple, functional and handsome, this bag epitomizes the craftsmanship and design of the Bill Amberg workshop.

BIBLIOGRAPHY

Art in Needlework Lewis F.Day, BT Batsford
1907

Handbags Anna Johnson, Workman Publishers
2002

Bags Clair Wilcox, Victoria & Albert Museum,
1999

Bags Pepin Press
2004

Attila and The Nomad Hordes David Nicolle,
Angus McBride Asprey Military Press
1990

Swords and Hilt Weapons Editor Anne Cope,
Weidenfeld and Nicholson
1989

Encyclopaedia Brittanica

In Vogue Georgina Howell, Penguin Books
1978

Lifework Norman Parkinson, Octopus Books
1986

Worldwide Web
www.wikipedia
www.random history
www.style.com
www.perfectlyvintage.co

Thanks to the following agencies and people for supplying pictures:
Getty Images, London, England
Mirco De Cet Archives, Newport, England
York Archaeological Trust for Excavation and Research Ltd, York, England
Topfoto Picture Library, Edenbridge, Kent, England
Dr Stephanie Lake—for supplying all Bonnie Cashin pictures.
Emilio Falchi, London, England
Corbis, London
Anya Hindmarch, London, England
Lulu Guinness, London England
Jamin Puech, Paris, France
The Bag Lady Emporium, USA   www.bagladyemporium.com
                              www.bagladyuniversity.com
Maroquinerie Delvaux, Bruxelles, Belgium
Kathrine Baumann, West Hollywood, Califormia, USA
Perfectly Vintage, Potters Bar, England   www.perfectlyvintage.co.uk
© Photo Korky Paul—Page 223
Emily Jo Gibbs—Page 246–247
Julie Guernsey, Los Angeles, USA (www.1860-1960.com)   Red Phone Bag—Page 305
DLM Deutsches Ledermuseum Schuhmuseum, Offenbach, Germany

Special thanks also to the following people and organisations for allowing us to photograph examples from their collections:
Tessa Paul
The Fashion Museum, Bath, England
Northampton Museum and Art Gallery, Northampton, England
Candy Says, Brentwood, England.   www.candysays.co.uk
Handbag Hire, Lincoln, England.   www.handbaghirehq.co.uk
Steptoes Dog Vintage Wears, Leeds, England. www.steptoesantiques.co.uk